THE GAIA ATLAS OF CITIES
New directions for sustainable urban living

THE GAIA ATLAS OF
CITIES

New directions for sustainable urban living

Herbert Girardet

Gaia Books Limited

a GAIA original

Conceived by
Joss Pearson

Written by
Herbert Girardet

Project consultants

John F. Charlewood Turner.
Pioneer since the 1950s in
promoting community-based housing and local development in both
Third and First World countries;
champion of the rights of people to
build, manage and sustain their own
shelter and communities; winner of
the Alternative Nobel Prize.

David Pearson, Dip. Arch., Lond.,
MRCP, UC Berkeley, RIBA.
Architect-planner trained in London
and as Harkness Fellow in Berkeley,
California. Consultant to Milton
Keynes New City and community
architect in London and Los Angeles.
Author of *The Natural House Book*
and founder of the *Ecological
Design Association.*

Project editor
Joanna Godfrey Wood

Editors
Fiona Trent
Suzy Boston

Project designer
Simon Adamczewski

Design development
Sara Mathews

Researcher
Chris Wilbert

Picture research
Susan Mennell

Direction
Joss Pearson
Patrick Nugent

Dedication

*To country people,
to city people,
and a living Earth
we must never
take for granted*

GAIA

® *This is a Registered Trade Mark
of Gaia Books Limited*

*Revised edition first published in the United Kingdom
in 1996 by Gaia Books Limited*

*66 Charlotte Street
London W1P 1LR*

and

*20 High Street
Stroud, Glos. GL5 1AS*

*A catalogue record for this book is available
from The British Library*

ISBN 1 85675 097 3

10 9 8 7 6 5 4 3 2 1

HABITAT II

UNITED NATIONS CONFERENCE, "THE CITY SUMMIT"

By Dr. Wally N'Dow, Secretary-General

In 1976, the UN held its first global conference on human settlements: Habitat I in Vancouver, Canada. At that time there was still hope that rapid urban growth could be mitigated or even diffused and the conference drew international attention to problems in settlements of all kinds, rural as well as urban. Now, in 1996, Habitat II builds on this effort and focuses on the urbanization process itself, as cities and town accommodate the majority of the world's population.

Humanity is facing two major unprecedented challenges, which are the main focus of Habitat II, the United Nations Conference on Human Settlements, "The City Summit", in Istanbul, Turkey, in June 1996:

● How can we provide adequate shelter and livelihoods for the world's ever-growing numbers of urban citizens?

● How can we achieve sustainable human settlements in an urbanizing world?

All photographs by Herbert Girardet

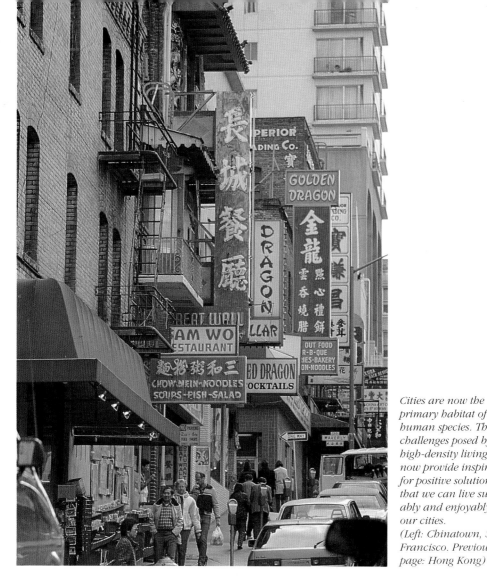

Cities are now the primary habitat of the human species. The challenges posed by high-density living must now provide inspiration for positive solutions, so that we can live sustainably and enjoyably in our cities.
(Left: Chinatown, San Francisco. Previous page: Hong Kong)

The human species is involved in an unprecedented stage in its evolution: it is turning itself into an urban species. Large cities, rather than villages and towns, are becoming our primary habitat. Not long after the new century dawns, half of humanity will live and work in cities and urban areas of all sizes, and the other half will depend more and more on them for their economic survival while continuing to live in villages and towns. Within a single century global urban populations will have expanded from 15 to 50 per cent, a figure that looks set to continue increasing.

The size of modern cities, in terms of numbers as well as physical scale, has never been seen before: in 1800, there was only one city on the planet that contained as many as a million people – London. At that time the 100 largest cities in the world altogether accommodated 20 million inhabitants, with each city covering an area of just a few thousand hectares.

In 1990, the world's 100 largest cities accommodated 540 million people and 220 million people lived in the 20 largest cities; megacities of over ten million people, each covering hundreds of thousands of hectares. In addition, there were 35 cities of over five million and hundreds containing over one million people.

In the 19th and early 20th centuries, urban growth was occurring mainly in the developed nations, as a result of the spread of industrialization and the associated rapid increase in the use of fossil fuels. Today, the world's largest and fastest-growing cities are emerging in the developing world, because of urban-industrial development, and as a consequence of rural decline.

City growth is changing the face of the earth and the very condition of humanity. Can the planet accommodate an urbanized human species, drawing its resources from an increasingly global hinterland? Can the human race cope with high levels of urban density, living solely in high-rise concrete canyons? Or, indeed, can it cope with urban sprawl, and with urban motorway networks stretching out over vast distances? Can planners, architects, administrators, and ordinary citizens create a sustainable and acceptable life in a world composed principally of large cities?

A point that is not made often enough is that cities provide major opportunities for sustainable development, given that they accommodate large numbers of people in a limited space. They offer significant economies of scale in the provision of jobs, housing, and services. We now need fully to realize the potential of cities for ecological, economic, and social sustainability. We must offer people security and comfort without destroying a healthy global environment on which all cities ultimately depend.

AN URBAN PLANET

The key issue we face today is the extraordinary speed of urban growth. Urban populations are increasing three times faster than overall populations – 4.7 as compared to 1.6 per cent – because of both rural-urban migration as well as the rapidly rising birth rate of urban populations in many parts of the world.

Humanity has only limited experience of life in large

cities, and lessons of how to run them sustainably are only just being learned. There is much talk about the "global urban crisis" of air and water pollution, lack of infrastructure, homelessness, unemployment, and traffic congestion. But there has been much less talk of the vast range of problem-solving initiatives under way in the world's cities, both in developed and developing nations. And there has not been enough information provided about the huge opportunities for governments at all levels, the private and non-governmental sectors all over the world, to work in partnership to creatively shape our urban future. The work of Habitat II in collating examples of urban "best practices" from all over the world is designed to fill that gap.

Central governments have realized that they alone cannot cope with the changes being brought about by rapid urbanization. Consequently, they are developing new forms of collaboration with local authorities, the private sector, non-governmental organizations and community groups. Many national governments have realized that local authorities need to play a stronger and more autonomous role if the goal of sustainable urban development is to be achieved.

Habitat II seeks to deepen the understanding of urban challenges and opportunities so that realistic steps can be taken at city, country, and international levels to develop new patterns of civic partnerships and governance to overcome urban problems and enrich the potentials of city life. There is certainly no shortage of the latter: cities are the home of human civilization, offering the prospect and platforms of economic development, educational opportunities, and cultural excellence.

As engines of economic development, cities act as magnets, causing rural-urban migration. By offering employment opportunities for vast numbers of people they turn rural people into city dwellers. Currently, this is particularly the case in countries of East Asia such as China, Thailand, Malaysia, and South Korea, where urban economic growth has reached previously unknown levels, affecting hundreds of millions of people. Urbanization there has dramatically increased standards of living, resulting in greater affluence in cities than in the country.

Meanwhile cities, as motors of economic growth, also affect living standards in rural areas. As better roads are built and access to urban products is assured, rural people acquire urban aspirations, with urban standards of living to match. Rural-urban migration also occurs as a result of the perception that cities offer better educational opportunities than rural areas. In addition, cities are seen as centres of culture and entertainment, offering a vast variety of choice for all tastes and preferences.

SHELTER: MORE THAN JUST A ROOF

To accommodate ever-growing numbers of new city dwellers the provision of adequate shelter for all is one of the major tasks ahead of us and the plight of the urban homeless is well-documented. Despite substantial initiatives in many of the world's great cities, both in the developed and the developing world, hundreds of millions of the urban poor are continuing to have to live without adequate homes. All citizens have a right to expect their governments to be concerned about adequate shelter and secure neighbourhoods.

Adequate shelter means much more than just having a roof over one's head. It also means privacy, adequate space and security, a place in which to thrive, the structural stability and durability of a dwelling with proper lighting and ventilation, and with an adequate infrastructure for sanitation and waste management. It is also important for shelter to be located close to work and basic facilities – all this at an affordable cost.

It has become apparent that a shared approach to shelter provision greatly contributes to sustainable settlements' development. This approach, which allows people to play a major role in the creation of their own homes, has proved to be a very efficient way of mobilizing resources and of giving people control and autonomy in their own lives. Examples from many countries, including Ethiopia, Zambia, Senegal, Peru, Colombia, Brazil, Thailand, India, and Pakistan, show that empowering communities to construct and upgrade their own homes is a cost-effective and self-empowering way of providing good, long-lasting homes for city-dwellers.

In addition, enabling housing markets to perform their function efficiently is another important strategy. Here, too, there are lessons from all over the world: the Housing Bank in Thailand is a case in point. By making it easy for people to borrow, the scheme facilitates the construction of hundreds of thousands of homes for lower middle class people. It shows how people's savings can be mobilized for their own benefit. As a result of such initiatives, cities such as Bangkok have been able to keep up with much of the high demand for good-quality, low-cost housing.

ENVIRONMENT: THE BIG ISSUE

Because of the demands cities make on the environment, they are centre-stage in the global environmental drama. The concentration of intense economic activity and the high levels of consumption among dense city populations both increase demands on natural resources by city-based activities. Built on two per cent of the world's land surface, they use over three-quarters of the world's resources and discharge similar amounts of waste. Urban wastes have local impacts but are also a problem of global dimension. So let us think of our cities as being part of the world's major environmental agenda and look to reorganizing them as part of the global problem-solving process.

The impacts of cities are felt locally and globally. Take air pollution: city populations, as the major users of energy, cause both regional and worldwide air pollution, with

In the future city sewage plants must change their main fuction from making human waste safe for disposal to nutrient-recovery for use in city food production. (Above: London)

dramatic impacts on health of people and the biosphere. On a local scale, forms of air pollution – consisting of nitrogen oxides, sulphur dioxide, carbon monoxide, particulates and unburnt hydrocarbons – is a problem in most of the world's great cities. Globally, a major issue is the increase of carbon dioxide in the atmosphere, now recognized as the major culprit in global warming.

Central and local governments are increasingly aware that efforts to improve the living environment must be focused on urban centres. Sustainable urban development is, therefore, the most pressing challenge facing humanity in the twenty-first century. Can the vast appetites of the cities for resources, and their huge waste discharges, be curtailed? Can they turn into a resource- and energy-efficient home for humanity? Can efforts to improve the environmental performance of our cities also create new opportunities for urban employment?

URBAN TECHNOLOGY: REDUCING THE FOOTPRINT

Urban growth in the last two centuries was only made possible by the use of a whole range of new technologies, such as fossil fuel-based transport, electricity and gas supply technologies, piped water supply and sewage, and solid waste disposal systems. Many of these technologies have continued largely unchanged over the last few decades. All too often they are now out of date in terms of the requirement for the environmentally sustainable urban development that we now consider as paramount.

Many of the environmental problems of cities are actually related to the use of urban technologies. Energy supply systems and transport systems are often highly inefficient, discharging inordinate amounts of waste gases. Our sewage systems, typically, do not place much emphasis on the recovery of valuable plant nutrients that ought to be returned to farmland where crops for urban consumption are grown. And too much solid waste is just dumped and not recycled into useful products. As a result, cities indulge in an excessive use of resources and, associated with this, produce an adverse environmental impact.

Today, we have a great opportunity to develop a whole new range of environmentally sound technologies for use in our cities. Efficient energy supply systems are now readily available, including combined heat-and-power generators, fuel cells and photovoltaic modules for electricity supply to urban buildings. New materials and concepts of architectural design allow us greatly to improve the energy performance of urban buildings, and reduce the poisonous impact of materials use, in buildings. And recycling technologies for small and large, rich and poor cities make possible greater efficiency in the urban use of resources. The task is to reduce the "footprint" of cities and to create an increasingly circular urban metabolism.

GENDER: EXPERIENCING CITIES DIFFERENTLY

Women and men use and experience cities differently according to their roles, responsibilities, and resources. Urban opportunity and urban disadvantage are experienced by both sexes, but women tend to bear a disproportionate burden of disadvantage. Many are mothers, community managers as well as income earners, often travelling great distances between home and work. Low-income women in developing-world cities are often particularly hard hit. When basic services are lacking, women commonly take on responsibilities such as water and fuel collection and refuse disposal. Often, they are involved in food and livestock production whilst having only limited security of land tenure.

But women all over the world are questioning the way responsibilities are distributed and cities are managed; many have formed vigorous pressure groups for changing the way cities are run. This has also led them to take a close look at the way cities are planned in terms of spatial arrangements. Women tend to have different perceptions of urban space than men, strongly emphasizing the importance of close proximity between home and place of work.

Overall, gender issues affect urban policies in a number of areas. For example, with changing lifestyles in which two-parent families are less usual in some cities, there is a growing realization that traditional urban structures separating the "private" world of the home from the "public" world of work and government are no longer conducive to modern-day living. The idea that the public world belongs to men and the private world belongs to women is no longer valid; yet today's urban structures fail to reflect this.

The fact is that urban planning is still gender-biased because women are still grossly under-represented in this field and because most urban planners often do not have data showing who does what and who benefits most. We must look forward to a situation in which women, men, boys and girls can all feel personally responsible for helping shape and develop their city and for the quality of life it offers all its citizens.

YOUTH: INHERITING AN URBAN FUTURE

Young people will inherit the urban future that is currently in the making. In many countries they constitute a very large proportion of urban populations. In 1992, world youth population was one-third of total world population. Out of this, 84 per cent lived in cities. Yet often young people face great uncertainties about employment, the stresses of urban growth and, in some instances, urban mismanagement. Many young people meet the sunset of their opportunities at the dawn of their existence, with unemployment and insecurity leading to crime, violence, and drug abuse. Yet they are entitled to a healthy and productive life of social peace and equal opportunities in harmony with the natural world.

It is therefore crucial for young people actively to participate in decision-making on issues that affect their lives today and in the future. This also means having a say in investments in education, training, and job creation that can affect their future positively. Their energy, intellectual capacity, and ability to muster support for urban initiatives is crucial for generating meaningful change.

URBAN FARMING: THE COMPLETED CIRCLE

In traditional cities urban agriculture was an important feature of urban life, contributing to regular food supplies as well as providing security in times of emergency. Many of the world's great cities continue supplying substantial amounts of food from within their territories, particularly to the poorer sectors of urban society in China, Africa, India, and Latin America. Urban vegetable growing has been making a comeback even in cities in the developed world such as New York. Urban farming is beneficial because it creates employment, reduces the cost of transportation, storage, and wholesale handling of food, whilst also ensuring freshness of supplies.

An interesting aspect of urban agriculture is its use of organic manures and compost, which are always readily available. Cairo has shown just how much food can be grown on urban fringe farms with compost from the city. The city's waste recyclers, widely recognized and supported for providing a valuable service to the city, have been equipped with the technology to compost large quantities of organic materials. All cities have a surplus of these materials and their proper use on urban or city fringe land in the growth of food for the city is an important aspect of long-term urban sustainability.

BEST PRACTICES: THE FIVE LESSONS

Only people can implement measures for sustainable urban development – technical fixes are not enough. A good knowledge base is crucial, so best practices worldwide must be collected and disseminated.

These are the five lessons which emerged during our preparatory work for Habitat II:

1. Spread the good news

There are many fascinating initiatives already taking place throughout the world's cities. Habitat and its partners have helped groups to prepare reports and to make films of these best practices and to disseminate them to interested parties. This process will help to widen knowledge and deepen the understanding of urban challenges and opportunities so that realistic steps can be taken at local, national, and international levels.

2. Simplify complex issues

Modern cities are complex organisms. This means successful implementation of initiatives must be analysed and effective processes for implementing projects identified at their simplest levels.

3. Tailor actions to local situations

How applicable are best practices when applied to cities outside their own regions? For urban best practices to be transferable from one city to another, implementation must be closely tailored to local situations.

4. Exchange people between cities

The sharing of best practices between cities is an essential tool for urban sustainable development. Once outside interest in a project has been established, site visits are of critical importance.

5. Change the way urban institutions work

Allowing people direct access to best practices through a process of decentralized co-operation is vital. Material collected in a central computerized data bank is a gold mine for all the world's cities to excavate.

By the time the next century passes its first quarter, more than a billion and a half people in the world's cities will face life- and health-threatening environments unless we create a revolution in urban problem-solving. The job cannot be done by telling the world what it already knows. We need a new approach, a creative and constructive effort that can only come if we forge a global partnership between national governments and local communities, between the public and private sectors alike.

Whether it is the environment or human rights, population or poverty, or the status of women, or the use of technology, we must deal with the issues in our human settlements. That is why they have become a priority challenge for the international community; why it is essential that they are at the centre of a growing global effort to make our cities and all communities productive, safe, healthy, more equitable, and sustainable.

A wise man once said: "The gift of material goods makes people dependent, but the gift of knowledge makes them free". Today, the gift of knowledge of how to heal our cities, how to make them sustainable on a rapidly urbanizing planet is the most urgent knowledge we, as a race, can acquire. The Habitat II agenda is designed to help spread that knowledge.

Cities in the developed world, such as New York, have learned from the developing world that good food can be successfully grown within the confines of the city, providing a green oasis amongst the concrete. (Below: The Bronx, New York)

"She has been looking at the external city; but the internal city is more important, the one that you construct inside your head. That is where the edifice of possibility grows, and grows without your knowledge; it is subject to no planner's control."

Hilary Mantel, *Eight Months On Ghazzah Street*

CONTENTS

World city, city world

The urban species

Sometime around the turn of the millennium an urban baby will be born whose birth will tip the balance statistically, for humanity, from being a predominantly rural into a predominantly urban species. In this culminating move to full urbanization, will humanity be fulfilling its destiny? Or will we be entering the final stage in decline toward chaos and collapse?

Cities and the planet's resources

The history of early cities shows that they often depleted local hinterlands, draining their fertility without replenishing it. They exhausted the forests, watersheds, and farmland that had enabled their existence. The ancient city sites of Mesopotamia are now surrounded by bleak wastelands, covered in crusts of salt. Are we repeating this tragedy today, but on a planetary scale? The world's large cities now have the whole planet as their hinterland; they draw on resources and dump their wastes all around the globe. How can we avoid turning the planet into a desert, as the majority of our rapidly multiplying humankind becomes urban-based?

It is the burgeoning cities' huge appetite for the world's resources, and the vast quantities of wastes they discard, that cause the greatest concern about their long-term viability. Few modern cities are, as yet, actually collapsing due to a breakdown of supplies. Science and industrial technology are attempting to ensure that the land from which cities get their food stays

Rickshaws
Congestion on the city streets is a major problem the world over. In developing-world cities, such as Dhaka, Bangladesh (left), jams are caused by hand carts, bicycles, and hand-drawn rickshaws rather than cars and lorries. Lack of air-polluting emissions mitigates the situation.

Cities as magnets
The rapid growth of cities has become the most striking feature of our civilization. There now seems little likelihood that this trend will be halted. Cities are predominantly human worlds and they have become irresistible magnets for people all over the planet.

productive, that technical solutions can be put into place when reliance on nature's bounty becomes less certain. But the technosphere, which props up modern urban living, has been established with little regard for the need to ensure an intact biosphere on which the well-being of all living things ultimately depends.

The limits of urban growth are increasingly seen as environmental. Yet the issue of how modern cities might achieve sustainability has rarely been properly addressed. Will the mega-cities, with their vast appetites, turn this into a ruined planet? Or can we find ways in which to consolidate urban growth and to make our cities sustainable?

The parasite and the host

It is time to take a rational look at the relation-ship, presently largely parasitic, between cities and their host environment. If we are to con-tinue to live in cities, indeed if we are to continue to flourish on this planet, we will have to find a viable relationship between cities and the living world – a relationship not parasitic but symbiotic, or mutually supportive. This book seeks to assess how this might be achieved. Part One looks at the way cities function – in terms of their metabolism, their communities, their climate and environs, their financial hold on the world, and their historical evolution. Part Two explores the problems that have arisen as a result of cities operating linear processes (see pp. 22-5). Part Three describes innovative schemes for "closing the circle"; making urban metabolisms circular, and healing cities again.

Can cities be sustainable?

Can an urbanized world be ecologically viable? This question concerns not only the appetite of

City scale
Human scale disappears beneath the pressures of numbers, growth, and the need to plan and organize our cities, turning them into grid-patterned mazes with "crystal" downtown centres (as in San Francisco, top left). Many smaller cities, especially in the developing world, still retain their spontaneous layouts and their human scale. The photograph bottom left shows Metlili in the Algerian Sahara, home of the Chaamba.

The urban mind change

The impact of cities is confined not only to environments from which they draw their resources. People, too, are changed profoundly as they are transformed from hunter-gatherers and peasants into urban factory and office workers. Intimate daily contact with the natural world is replaced by routine encounters with a world of bricks, concrete, and tarmac. A new way of life emerges as people give up local rural self-sufficiency for dependence on resources and products from distant places. By becoming supermarket hunter-gatherers, exchanging money for deep-frozen and packaged food, by spending our time in sealed build-ings insulated from encounters with nature, we tend to forget that the integrity of the living world is of key importance for our own future wellbeing.

City markets

Worldwide (here in Bombay, above left, and New York, above), city markets have always been places where people meet to buy and sell and to socialize – they are part of the hub of city life. But modern technology threatens this vital contact.

cities for raw materials and manufactured goods but also the wastes and pollution they release into the world. Cities, as centres of consumption of food, fuel, timber, and all kinds of factory-made products, have huge waste-disposal problems. Our current attitude – out of sight, out of mind – is the most convenient response. But it is also a particularly short-sighted one. In sewers and waste dumps we mix poisonous materials with those that could be used to enhance the fertility of farmland. Solid wastes end up in local landfills as well as in toxic waste dumps half-way around the world. The liquid wastes of cities pollute rivers and coastal waters. Air pollution from different cities meets and merges together, covering the planet with a veil of waste gases, a new feature of the Earth's atmosphere commented on by astronauts.

The appropriate way to deal with scarce resources is prudent consumption. More efficient functioning of cities could also ensure a reduction of wastes. What we do discard needs to be recycled, as part of a circular process. Separation of materials before they are discarded can ensure that recycling becomes viable and realistic. That way we stand a much better chance of achieving the goal of making cities sustainable.

Global co-operation

The lines of supply of modern urban production systems are difficult to comprehend. Yet we need to understand their implications if we are to achieve a sustainable urban way of life. Our worldwide communication systems enable us to gain an understanding of global impact. Cities are the hubs of these communications systems. They should enable us to grasp what is at stake and to act accordingly.

Popular concern and participation is a critical precondition for reducing the damage cities are doing to far-flung places. Cities are organisms, with an evolutionary history, a life of their own, and clearly identifiable consumption patterns. The citizens who create them need to recognize and take responsibility for these patterns. Unlike countries, cities are definable structures, whose inputs and outputs can be precisely measured. They are units more easily tackled when it comes to reorganizing their consumption and discharge. One way of achieving this is global co-operation. Today city people can easily collaborate with other communities in distant places. Acting globally cities can work with people in remote regions to help prevent environmental damage far away. Working together, cities can guard the functioning of the biosphere, on which cities ultimately depend.

Taking responsibility

One thing is clear: cities are here to stay for as long as they can and it is critical for them to stop being centres of human self-advancement. Instead they need to take responsibility for their impact on the planet and to learn how they can become compatible with all living species and the natural world. The future of Gaia depends on it.

Cars
Rush-hour traffic jams (such as this one, right, in San Francisco) are now a common experience on the roads, streets, and motorways of developed- and developing-world cities alike. Polluting emissions from cars threaten human and plant life both in cities and the wider world.

Cities as cancers
Not everyone is convinced of the attraction of cities. Wherever someone has praised cities as centres of culture and human endeavour, someone else has called them cancers on the face of the Earth. Wherever someone talks of the triumph of cities, someone else talks about their fragility and uncertain future.

PART ONE

The ecology of settlements

Cities are the single most complex products of the human mind. Their labyrinthine street plans are the most intricate human designs to appear on the face of the Earth, becoming the mind maps of their inhabitants. Cities are more than static structures of stone and concrete. They are also vast processors of food, fuels, and the many raw materials that feed a civilization. With their complex metabolisms they are huge organisms without precedent in nature; their connections stretch across the globe. But fossil fuel technology has brought a quantum leap in urban development, producing cities that extend over vast distances. The megacities of today have evolved without instruction manuals. Can they be turned into benign organisms?

"One was either in or out of the city; one belonged or one did not belong. When the town gates were locked at sundown, and the portcullis was drawn, the city was insulated from the outside world. As in a ship, the wall helped create a feeling of unity between the inhabitants."

Lewis Mumford, *The Culture of Cities*

CHAPTER 1

The dynamic city

The city throughput
Modern cities have their own inner climates, different from their hinterlands (see pp. 28-9), they are often homes to surprising inhabitants (see pp. 30-1), and their locations can be unexpected (see pp. 32-3). But their main role, as giant processors of raw materials, is possibly more intriguing than any of these: cities are continuous converters of materials into artificial objects. All cities have massive throughputs of resources, mostly imported from elsewhere: anywhere. The concept of the "metabolism" of cities (see pp. 22-5) enables us accurately to assess their regular demands for food, water, raw materials, and fuels, and the potential impact of their use and processing on the biosphere. The inefficiency of the current, linear metabolism of cities is of staggering proportions and threatens to affect the wellbeing of Gaia.

Cities control and mould
Modern cities are also concentrations of money and power (see pp. 34-5). By financing the transformation and processing of raw materials into consumer products cities try to transcend nature and establish a continually changing man-made world. By combining and processing nature's materials into artefacts, cities are undermining natural limitations with, as yet, uncertain environmental consequences. Because of the ferocious power to control and mould the world within their reach there is now an urgent necessity to "tame" our modern cities.

The human role
Modern urbanism also means a complex division of labour, utilizing vast reservoirs of human creativity. Somehow cities manage to motivate their inhabitants to play their own unique role in a world in which they are all centre stage. Today this complex urban world is not confined to individual cities. A global network of cities is emerging which enables people to link up with each other over vast distances in trade and the exchange of ideas. The "global village" is giving rise to "globalopolis" (see pp. 36-7).

Organism or machine?

Cities have been described both as "organisms" and as "mechanisms". Seen as organisms, cities convert raw materials into products and waste, energizing themselves in the process. The urban organism seeks to reproduce the living conditions necessary for human survival. Seen as mechanisms, cities seek to transcend biological limits. They are artificial structures depending on transport systems and factories to function, producing objects alien to the natural world.

The city machine
Cities transform raw materials into finished products (below right). They convert food, fuels, forest products, minerals, water, and human energy, into buildings, manufactured goods, and financial and political power: all the components of civilization. This refining process has radically altered the world. Cities dominate human affairs and their demands are beginning to outstrip the capacity of the planet.

Inventiveness

Work

Food

Raw materials

Energy

Culture

Manufacturing

The city jungle and market place
As concrete jungles (left) cities practice the survival of the fittest but also co-operation and mutual aid. As global markets (centre left) they control the world's products.

Political power

Products

Waste

"Civilization"

Supplying cities' needs

Land on which cities are built cannot support the high density of their urban populations. They have always been dependent on essential supplies of food, timber, firewood, and water from their hinterlands. Cities, as centres of consumption, have the potential for doing great environmental damage, but never more than now, when they are drawing on supplies from global hinterlands.

Today the demand for supplies from cities is much more complex than ever before. A huge variety of inputs is required to keep them going and fossil fuels are top of the shopping list. Modern cities are homes to people who take a lifestyle amplified by fossil-fuel-powered technology for granted. Long-distance transport that brings in food and raw materials, with its further squandering of resources, is part of that scenario. If supplies of food from their surrounding countryside suddenly ceased, modern cities would not necessarily collapse, as did some of their ancient predecessors (see pp. 40-1). They have access to food and other supplies from all over the world.

Biocidic cities

Many cities in history have taken essentials without giving anything in return. They have taken food without returning fertility to the soil; they have taken forest products without contributing to reforestation; they have taken water without ensuring sustainable supplies. Such cities have thus undermined their own existence, and ultimately caused their own demise (see pp.42-3). Dusty ruins, surrounded by wasteland, are all that remain of once-thriving Ur and Babylon. Is the same being done by modern cities, but this time on a global scale?

Biogenic cities

Some cities of the past took great care to replenish the land that gave them their food and timber. The Chinese were keenly aware of the need to return human and animal waste to the land. Traditional Chinese culture respected the cycles of nature and saw the need for humans to live accordingly. The cities of China to this day return human waste to the belt of farmland that surrounds them, and which is maintained by them (see pp. 162-3). Despite a population of 12.5 million Shanghai, and other cities like it, are nearly self-sufficient in vegetables

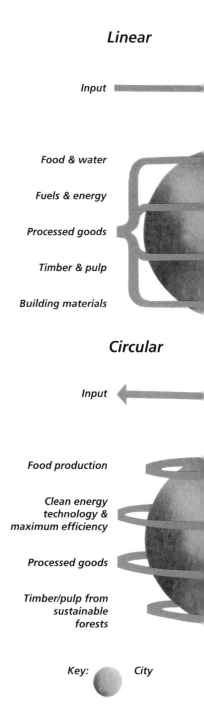

Linear

Input

Food & water

Fuels & energy

Processed goods

Timber & pulp

Building materials

Circular

Input

Food production

Clean energy technology & maximum efficiency

Processed goods

Timber/pulp from sustainable forests

Key: City

metabolism

Output

Sewage

Exhaust gases

Household &
factory wastes:
liquid & solid

Wanton disposal

metabolism

Output

Plant nutrient
recycling

Sulphur & nitrogen
oxide interception

Recycled goods
(with minimum
pollution)

Large-scale
tree planting
(uptake of CO_2)

Throughput

and grain. However, now that China is the world's leading burner of coal – much of it containing high concentrations of acid-producing sulphur – the ecological viability of Chinese cities is being reduced.

Linear metabolism

A city with a linear metabolism takes what it needs from a vast area, with no thought for the consequences, and throws away the remains. Input is unrelated to output. Nutrients are removed from the land as food is grown, never to be returned. Timber is felled for building purposes or pulp without reforestation occurring. Raw materials are extracted, combined, and processed into consumer goods, resulting in rubbish that cannot be beneficially reabsorbed into nature. Fossil fuels are mined in unprecedented quantities or pumped out from the rock strata and refined, burned, and released into the atmosphere. In sum, our present urban-industrial civilization is accelerating environmental destruction with, as yet, hardly imagined consequences for the future of life on the planet.

Circular metabolism

For cities to be ecologically viable their functioning needs to be rethought and reorganized. In a city with a circular metabolism every output can also be used as an input into the production system, thereby affecting a far smaller area. Sewage systems cease being disposal systems for the noxious mixture of household and factory liquid wastes. Toxic liquid wastes are kept separate from "valuable" household sewage and washing powders, cleaners, and bleaches are fully biodegradable. Sewage works are designed to function as fertilizer factories rather than as disposal systems for unwanted, often poisonous, discharges. Liquid chemical wastes from factories are treated separately or no longer used, encouraging companies to invest in recycling technology and non-toxic production processes. Household and factory rubbish is regarded as an asset rather than an encumbrance and recycling is integral to the functioning of cities rather than an optional "add on" feature.

Responsible energy systems

Cities cannot exist without substantial energy inputs. But most energy supplies are fraught with environmental hazards: firewood, coal, and oil all have their own problems of extraction and pollution. The combustion of natural gas, while producing less carbon dioxide (CO_2) than coal, still has the associated climatic dangers of global warming and rising sea levels (see pp. 112-13). The nuclear option for "assured" energy supplies for cities is now considered seriously by an ever-smaller number of energy planners.

It is clear, therefore, that a combination of energy efficiency and clean energy technology is critical for the sustainability of our cities. Vast improvements in the energy performance of cities are feasible with current technologies. Solar technologies are making giant strides and it is no longer inconceivable for urban houses to be able to supply their own energy needs by a combination of solar water heating and photo-voltaic systems (see pp. 142-5).

Our transport systems, too, are unsustainable. The reliance on the private car is putting a heavy strain on urban environments as well as the biosphere. Cities, to become sustainable, require transport policies discouraging routine use of cars. Reorganization of city layouts, with greater proximity between home, work, and shops is a top priority. Without efficient transport systems cities cannot improve their all-important resource efficiency.

Cities' responsibility for forests

Strategies for the responsible combustion of fossil fuels must involve cities in taking action to enhance the planet's vegetation cover. Only vast areas of healthy forests can absorb the surplus carbon dioxide that the cities of developed and developing countries will release in the foreseeable future. Reforestation over an area of 1 million square kilometres will absorb 1 billion tonnes of CO_2, which is up to one quarter of the net annual build-up in the atmosphere (see pp. 112-13). Increasing the world's forest cover, rather than depleting it further, is critical for an urban society that takes the use of fossil fuel combustion for granted. But in most parts of the world land is already used for other purposes. Reforestation can, therefore, only take place with the help, and taking into account the needs, of local communities the world over.

The footprint of cities

The Canadian economist William Rees has defined the "ecological footprint of cities" as the land required to feed them, to supply them with timber products and to reabsorb their CO_2 emissions by areas covered with growing vegetation. Defined in this way London, with 12 per cent of Britain's population, and extending to 170,000 ha, has a footprint of some 21 million ha, or about 125 times its surface area, amounting to the entire productive land of the UK.

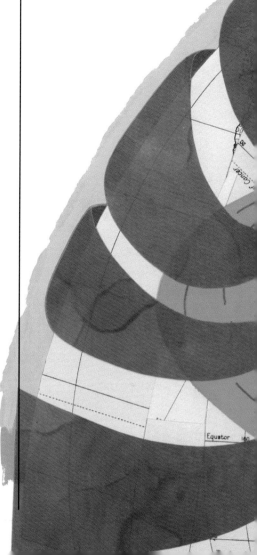

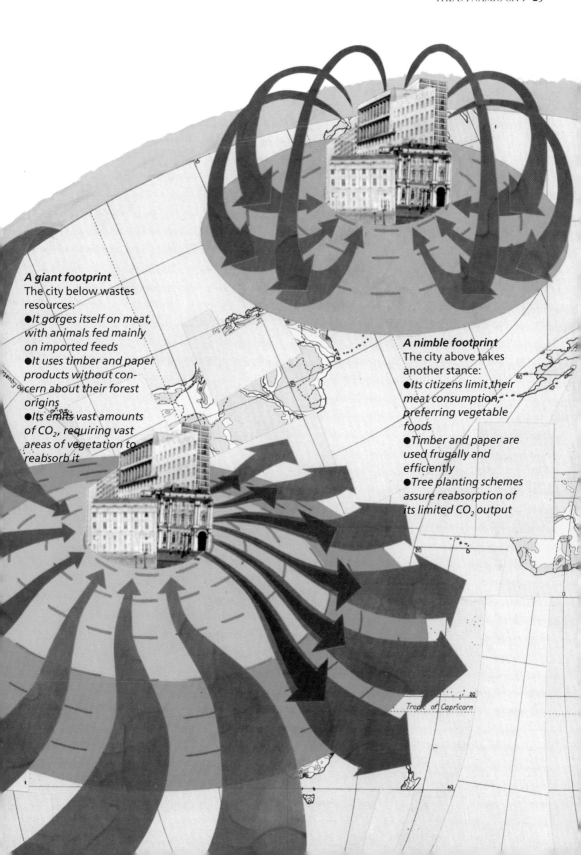

A giant footprint
The city below wastes resources:
● It gorges itself on meat, with animals fed mainly on imported feeds
● It uses timber and paper products without concern about their forest origins
● Its emits vast amounts of CO_2, requiring vast areas of vegetation to reabsorb it

A nimble footprint
The city above takes another stance:
● Its citizens limit their meat consumption, preferring vegetable foods
● Timber and paper are used frugally and efficiently
● Tree planting schemes assure reabsorption of its limited CO_2 output

Tropic of Capricorn

Lack of assessment

Few modern cities have assessed the implications of the way they affect the rest of the planet, taking for granted regular supplies of food and raw materials and the ability to discard their wastes. City administrations and urban populations have made little effort to conceptualize a sustainable, circular metabolism.

Consumption levels

The pioneering study by S. Boyden et al, "The Metabolism of Hong Kong", 1981, was a unique analysis of one city's metabolism. With a population of just under four million the city was, and is, a centre of light industry, with 60 per cent of its exports in textiles and clothing. The city already had many of the attributes of modern consumerism: 90 per cent of people had a television. In 1971 21 tonnes of building materials per head of population were incorporated in buildings and the transport network. A total of 87MJ (megajoules) per person of energy was used per day, which was one-sixth of the consumption of developed countries and three times more than that of developing countries. Annually 2.39 million tonnes of plant nutrients entered the Hong Kong food supply system: just over half a tonne per person per year.

Waste disposal

In 1971 the annual output of waste gases in Hong Kong was 255,000 tonnes, about six times less than a more sprawling city with the same population in a developed country. Annually waterborne sewage solids amounted to 2.3 million tonnes, 80 per cent of which was pumped untreated into Victoria Harbour. Daily the city discharged 2850 tonnes of solid waste, 0.7kg per person.

What does this study tell us?

The importance of this study is that it looks at the urban organism in the context of the capacity of the planet to fulfil our demands. The balance sheet of urban consumption does not list actual losses suffered by the biosphere: the time has come to assess the sustainability of current urban lifestyles.

The metabolism of Hong Kong

Hong Kong (below) has the densest concentration of people on the planet. High-rise living is the rule and people have managed to adapt. A surprisingly large amount of the city's food is actually produced within the colony's territory. But the city, departing from traditional Chinese practice (see pp. 162-3), is pumping most of its sewage into the sea, wasting valuable plant nutrients that could refertilize the land.

This unique study (see chart right) is a balance sheet for the metabolism of a city. Outgoings are not matched by income from renewable resources and the city, like most others, lives off nature's capital without it being renewed. Cities have yet to learn how to balance their books and invest in their future.

	INPUTS	OUTPUTS	
Metric tonnes per day		Exports	Waste
Human food	5985	602	
Animal food	335		
Food refuse			393
Fresh water	1,068,000		
Sea water	3,600,000		
Sewage liquids			819,000
Sewage solids			6301
Cargo	18,000	8154	
Liquid fuels	11,030	612	
Solid fuels	193	140	
Glass	270	65	152
Plastics	680	324	184
Cement	3572	11	
Wood	1889	140	637
Iron & steel	1878	140	65
Paper	1015	97	691
Other refuse			728
O_2	27,000		
CO			155
CO_2			26,500
SO_2			308
NO_x			110
C_xH_x			29
Particulates			42
Airborne lead			0.34

City heat dome

Urban heat islands

Cities are artificial heat islands frequently several degrees warmer than the surrounding countryside. This happens because of three main factors. First cities trap and store the sun's heat in roof tiles, stone surfaces, asphalt, and concrete and then release it back into the ambient air. Secondly cities are centres of energy consumption; in developed countries between 5 and 10 kilowatts of energy are used day and night for every person. Vehicles, electrical appliances, and light bulbs all give off heat, and air-conditioners work by cooling air inside buildings while discharging heat outside. Thirdly cities give off waste gases and dust. Carbon dioxide (CO_2) and nitrogen oxides (NOx), released by the combustion of fossil fuels, both act as greenhouse gases, which build up in the layers of air above cities.

Artificial heat generation

The greatest generation of artificial heat is usually in densely built-up city centres. Office buildings, apartment blocks, and factories all consume huge amounts of energy and discharge heat. Urban waste heat is between 1 and 10 per cent of incoming solar radiation. The heat emitted from urban sprawl equals 5 per cent of net incoming solar energy: the figure for Los Angeles is 6 per cent and rising. But peak figures can be much higher: in central Sydney artificial heat generation was found to be 50 per cent of incoming solar radiation on 12 days in July 1988.

Weather patterns

Urban waste heat in conjunction with dust particles can enhance rainfall. In Turin and Naples a distinct increase in light, frequent showers has been observed, while in Chicago weekday rainfall has been found to be greater than at weekends. Temperature differences can also contribute to wind turbulence, particularly in the angular, artificial canyons of towerblock landscapes. High urban temperatures can enhance air circulation causing buoyant, warm air to rise above the city centres and circulate outward toward the rural periphery. Meanwhile cooler country air flows into the city beneath the warm air.

The artificial urban heat "dome", caused by a combination of factors (see list right), occurs to a greater or lesser extent in all large cities. But the situation is worsened if the city is surrounded or backed by hills and mountains. These trap rising hot air and make its dispersal difficult. Highly polluted air, common in cities such as Athens, Los Angeles, and Mexico City, adds to the problem because the air cools and condenses around pollution particles, soot, and dust, causing frequent light rains and unpleasant smog – which can be a cumulative health risk.

The inner climate

● Solar radiation heats up air and makes it circulate

● CO_2 and NOx in the air act as greenhouse gases

● Concrete and tarmac store heat, adding to ambient temperature. Concrete canyons act as funnels, increasing wind speeds

● Air conditioning increases ambient temperatures

● Mirrored glass reflects solar radiation, adding to heat build-up

● Running engines give off heat through exhaust

● Warm sea breezes add to ambient heat of coastal cities

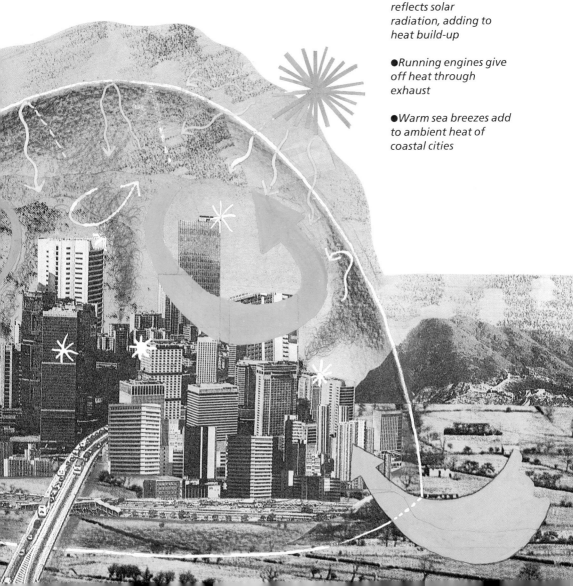

The city-makers

Landscapes into manscapes

As cities grow they try to claim landscapes for themselves, changing them gradually into "manscapes". When human settlements take centre stage, forests and farms are forced to give way as the green world is submerged under layers of tarmac and concrete. Newly built cities are usually wildlife deserts: monocultures of houses and uniform lawns with exotic conifers as living sculptures.

Nature reasserts itself

Yet wildlife joins with humanity in the making of the city. As time passes cracks appear in the concrete and vegetation finds a way of reasserting itself in the habitat, which is not as hostile as it first seemed. As cities mature they can even become wildlife refuges in their own right. Derelict gardens, crumbling walls, cemeteries, and embankments harbour plants and animals that have been driven close to extinction on impoverished, pesticide-sprayed wheat prairies and rye grass monocultures that surround our cities.

Cities may appear to be accumulations of buildings, but they are also gardens and forests. In Europe 50 per cent of urban areas are green spaces. The seeds dropped by vegetation feed a variety of small birds and there are innumerable forgotten places where mosses, wild roses, and rare flowers make their appearance, followed by many kinds of insects, butterflies, and small mammals. In London 314 vertebrate species have been found within a radius of 32km from the centre.

Picking up the crumbs

Cities are places where great quantities of food are consumed and discarded by people, encouraging certain species to make their home there. North American cities are home to a greater number of birds than the surrounding countryside. Starlings, mainly urban dwellers now, have become the world's second most numerous bird, themselves having become food for hawks, kestrels, and owls. Herring gulls, magpies, and crows find rubbish tips convenient feeding grounds, while dustbins attract foxes and badgers.

City-dwellers would never be able to get rid of their fellow urban inhabitants even if they wanted to, as anyone who has ever seen weeds push up through a crack in tarmac will know. But even if city-living suits them birds and animals can find it difficult to comprehend the city, particularly at night, when there is a permanent "dawn" of orange street lights. In London the spring dawn chorus can go on all night and all winter.

"Long live the weeds and the wilderness yet."

Gerard Manley Hopkins

". . . the urban environment is a patchwork of many habitats. The relative numbers, distribution and diversity of animals and birds in various parts of the city are directly related to the diversity and structure of vegetation, which determine habitat quality."

Michael Hough *City Form & Natural Process,* 1989

Manhattan
A peregrine falcon (below) waits for its prey above the canyons of the city, which can often yield more food than the hinterland beyond.

The establishment of cities

An assured food supply is the foundation of rural settlements, but throughout the world prosperous villages have expanded beyond the limitations of agricultural self-sufficiency into enterprising towns. Once established, their inhabitants seek to transcend basic subsistence, and to develop "urbane" lifestyles that override local limitations. Towns and cities have always been hubs of trade, first in items such as salt or olive oil, and later in industrial products. Control over access to resources has made cities into manufacturing centres capable of transforming the natural world.

Competitive cities

Trade and industry are the life blood of towns and cities. An ever-greater division of labour meets the needs and desires of customers wanting ever-more sophisticated goods, bringing never-ending innovation and change. The wealth of cities generates a jealous desire on the part of other cities to compete for markets. Cities, not the countryside, the world over are both trading partners and competitors of other cities, where wealth and power is located.

Power and vulnerability

By transcending the location and natural base from which they spring, cities are highly artificial creations, vulnerable to the very change they initiate. Innovation, by definition, creates impermanence. Today's cities, with their dependence on fossil fuels, are in turn dependent on global supplies that are susceptible to disruption and price inflation. Trade and manufacturing are impermanent states, too, subject to disruption and changing market conditions. They should not be allowed to dominate the life of cities to the detriment of the land on which they are built. Urban growth often takes place on fertile farmland, undermining the capacity of cities to feed themselves. All cities will one day stagnate and they must plan for that eventuality. It is therefore crucial for them to maintain a viable ecological base, nourishing, not undermining, the fertility of local farmland and rivers.

The logic of location

Early cities established themselves on fertile land, on fish-rich rivers, on lakes and oceans, on trade routes, near ore, coal, or oil deposits, and on holy sites. But the origin of cities was not their destination. Trade and industry caused cities to transcend their original reason for being as they turned fossil fuels and resources into goods, money, and power.

New York
Dutch, then British, port; now North America's cultural, commercial, and financial capital

Los Angeles
Founded by Spanish in 1781; now financial centre set in rich farmland, courtesy of water pipelines

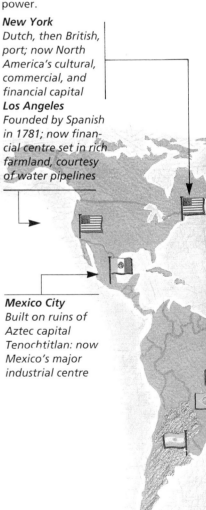

Mexico City
Built on ruins of Aztec capital Tenochtitlan: now Mexico's major industrial centre

Red areas indicate countries with at least 40% of total population living in capital city

Rio de Janeiro
French Huguenot settlement before being taken by the Portuguese. Brazil's second largest city

São Paulo
Surrounded by agricultural hinterland: now produces a quarter of Brazil's GNP

Beijing
China's capital for 600 years: China's second largest city

Tianjin
Important seaport and transport centre for northern China

Shanghai
China's greatest seaport and industrial centre

Tokyo-Yokohama
12th-century Edo (Tokyo) was built on rich farmland and Yokohama was a small fishing village. Now world's largest agglomeration

Osaka
Ancient agricultural and religious centre, now Japan's second industrial centre

London
Capital city since C14th, becoming worlds first super-city in C19th

Moscow
Capital until 1712 and again from 1918. Centre of industry, trade, and transport

Seoul
Founded 600 years ago: capital and commercial and cultural centre of South Korea

Manila
Founded 400 years ago by the Spanish. With 13% of population it produces 33% of GDP

Delhi
Fought over by successive dynasties: New Delhi built as a capital by the British

Bombay
India's largest city and port on the Arabian sea, originally built on two off-shore islands

Buenos Aires
World's leading meat exporter, grew after railways were built to Pampas

Cairo
Egypt's capital for 1000 years, located on rich farmland

Calcutta
Founded by the British as trade port; still chief port and industrial centre of eastern India

Jakarta
Dutch colonial settlement: now Indonesia's capital and largest city.

The ecology of money

The financial clout of cities

Cities are centres of financial power that can profoundly affect life in distant places. International bank headquarters are the control towers of the global economy; their investment decisions can make the economies of distant countries take off or crashland, create markets for their commodities or put them out of business. Futures and stock market manipulations can determine whether forests are exploited or left in peace, and whether minerals are mined or allowed to stay in the ground.

Capital investments in new production facilities can make established producers redundant. Steel mills in Duisburg and shipyards in Glasgow were closed down as those in Seoul or Kuala Lumpur attracted capital injections because they were producing more economically. Old industrial cities fade as others, often half a world away, become the new factory towns.

Transient homes

Cities the world over vie with each other for financial power, but they are also the transient homes of footloose international capital. With global communications and computer networks, the power of financial centres to respond to new opportunities and to make the quick million is greater than ever. But so is the temptation to do so at any price.

The hidden cost to nature

Money has no ecological consciousness. If timber from a virgin tropical forest is cheaper than a sustainable equivalent in Scandinavia then it will be hard to stop its extraction. The level of timber prices in the urban markets in the developed countries can thus determine the survival or destruction of unique wildlife habitats. Environmental damage is still not included in the price of the goods and food (see also pp. 92-3) we buy.

Many investment decisions are made for the supposed benefit of the urban consumer. To keep the urban economy ticking over and to sustain demand, prices have to be low and profit margins calculated tightly. Profitability is the name of the game that cities, and urban citizens, continue to play.

Cities such as Tokyo, New York, São Paulo, London, Hong Kong, and Mexico City house the headquarters of banks and multinational corporations: they are the centres of financial power and have come to dominate the global economy. A trillion dollars is probably on the move at any one time; billions can be added to or wiped off commodity prices or share values as the Earth completes one circuit of the sun.

Electronic link-up
Transactions between cities around the globe (right) are taken for granted. The daily financial merry-go-round starts in Tokyo, continues in London, and ends in New York and Los Angeles.

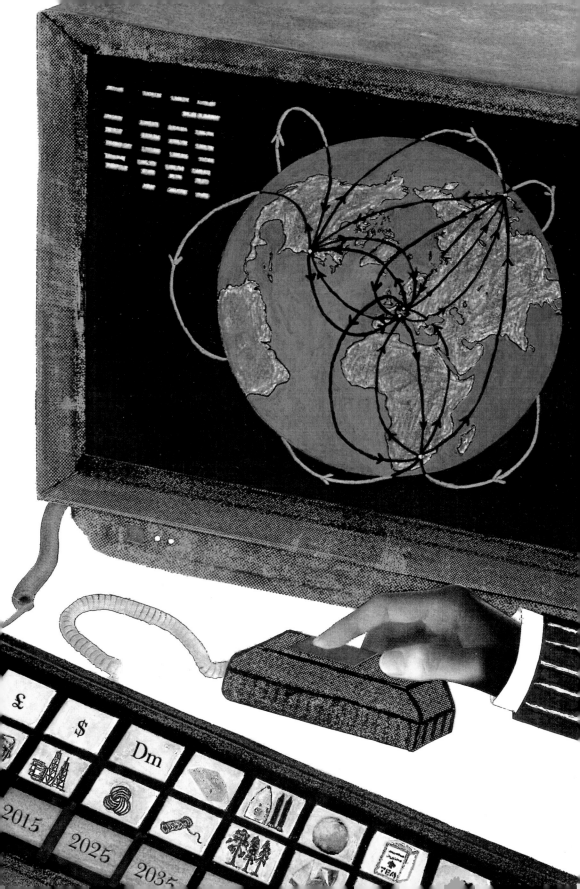

A global nervous system

The impacts of our way of life, with its enormous use of resources and its supply of foodstuffs from distant places, demands of us a global understanding of the impact of our consumption and discharge patterns. As modern urban citizens we think we can no longer live off local resources. Modern cities, by the very fact that they import materials from far and wide, have an effect on those places. It is our responsibility as urban citizens to find out what those impacts are. Computer networks can greatly help with this task; they have become a component of the nervous system of our new, global way of life and are now widely used to link environmental groups, planning joint action on important global issues such as rainforest destruction, air pollution or toxic waste trade. Television documentaries on major environmental issues can achieve a similar aim, making us aware of the effects of our day-to-day consumption patterns.

Acting locally?

The tentacles of modern urban economies stretch right around the globe. How can we best respond to this reality? The 1960s generated the slogan "think globally, act locally", which was widely quoted because it gave people a feeling of empowerment. For example, we could respond to the global climatic impact of carbon dioxide (CO_2) emissions by reducing energy consumption and increasing energy efficiency locally. A growing number of cities have set up projects to reduce their energy wastage (see pp. 142-5). The International Council for Local Environmental Initiatives was formed specifically for the purpose of municipalities all over the world to inform each other about environmental action. Fourteen cities in six countries have come together in a joint initiative to exchange information on improved local environmental practices.

Local action is important, but is no longer enough to cope with the global dimensions of our lifestyles. Today we need to take wider responsibilities, acting globally as well as locally. Even if we reduce the release of waste gases from individual cities, for example, their build-up in the atmosphere will continue from elsewhere. The inevitable continued release of substantial quantities of CO_2 demands a global response. Some environmental groups now suggest that we city people should all contribute to

Global co-operation over the telephone line

Computer networks do not only benefit people with power. In the 1980s, informal electronic networks for anyone with access to a computer, a modem, and a telephone line were set up in the world's major cities, allowing people to campaign globally on environmental issues of shared concern. Participating organizations included: GreenNet in Britain, EcoNet in North America, ComLink in Germany, GlasNet in Russia, WorkNet in South Africa, and Pegasus in Australia. These instant global communications form the basis for the development of a planetary "nervous system", able to respond to the worldwide power of our industrial civilization.

appropriate reforestation projects somewhere on Earth, which could help to soak up surplus CO_2 from the atmosphere.

Global village or globalopolis?

Another concept born in the 1960s that needs re-examining is the "global village", a term coined by the information theorist Marshall McLuhan. Since we are able to watch each other's way of life on television we can drop into living rooms on the other side of the world and learn to respect other people's lifestyles. We are all inhabitants of one global village, or so the theory goes.

But the reality is different. Villages, by definition, are small places where one gets to know other villagers intimately, by association with them year after year. Modern communications, at best, allow us to catch only a fleeting glimpse of one another. Of the 5.4 billion people on the planet, how many of those is one person likely to be acquainted with? The very complexity and anonymity of the modern world has given it an urban feel. Watching television reports of distant places is like sitting on a bus travelling through a city, glimpsing other people's living rooms as we drive past their windows. This is "globalopolis" rather than global village.

The people of Berlin, Singapore, Cairo, Nairobi, and Paris have more in common with one another than with the people who live in the rural areas near these cities. Urban people the world over share similar experiences of a man-made world of reinforced concrete, tarmac, glass, and bricks. Most cities have streets laden with traffic, with all the fumes and noise pollution that this implies. Cities usually have mixed populations, groups of people who have come together from many, often far afield, places, trying to make sense of living together and often achieving a better record of tolerance and peaceful co-existence of disparate groups than rural villages do.

"Globalopolis" could also be used as a term for the global power and reach of cities. They communicate with each other, electronically as well as physically, and many urban people are now, thanks to global transport systems, increasingly familiar with cities all over the world. A shared experience of urban living can contribute to shared responses to the global problems of urbanization.

"Many of the problems which confront us today are now global in scale, and to many of us they seem to be beyond our meagre resources. ... The Global Action Plan for the Earth is an attempt to break through this limitation in consciousness. ... The first step in our plan is to provide for people around the world a set of goals for areas of environmental achievement for the year 2000. ... The second part of the plan is to provide people with ... a communication feedback system to show people – at whatever they are operating – just how much their actions have contributed to a global effort. The third important part of our plan is to give people the skills to go out into the world and lead this new raising of environmental awareness."

Nadia McLaren, Oslo, quoted in *Ecocity*, 1990

CHAPTER 2
From settlements to cities

Growth and decline
Cities are at the heart of civilization: the organization of people in an urban way of life that we now take for granted. But until 10,000BC all people on earth lived in impermanent camps; they were gatherers and hunters of food – they harvested, but did not sow. The "neolithic revolution" turned nomads into settled farmers. The management of land was a new cultural departure, making humans into dominant creatures. With the growth of agriculture more permanent villages started to appear. The first towns such as Cathal Huyuk and Jericho appeared some 8000 years ago. The deliberate act of piling up structures of stone on an unsuspecting landscape was a new beginning for humankind.

Towns and cities are symbols of "order". By building permanent cities people tried to impose their will on the world. But today many early towns and cities are little more than heaps of stone and pottery fragments, having exhausted the land that fed them or having fallen into ruin after repeated wars with jealous neighbours (see pp. 40-1). Growth and decline permeates urban history. An understanding of this history is particularly valuable today as humanity is about to become a predominantly urban species.

The city 2000 years ago
In AD100 Rome was the world's largest city. In order to feed itself "the eternal city" drew on resources from further and further afield, depleting forests and farmland within the reach of its fleet (see pp. 42-3). Rome's fall was due both to the decline of the forests and farmland, and to the demise of its mercenary army, the reluctant guarantor of its overstretched supply lines. Like Rome, today's large cities get their food and energy supplies from distant places. Never before have cities depended on more vulnerable overseas sources of vital supplies.

After the fall of Rome and its centralized empire a new decentralized Europe emerged. Its mainly rural towns grew out of the fertility of local forests and farmland, which their inhabitants made efforts to keep productive. Like Chinese cities, Europe's medieval towns were sustainable urban systems

Symbols of order

The shapes of both houses and settlements reflected the order of man in the image of the cosmos. Circular settlements predominate in societies living close to nature, for example in the village forms of nomadic pastoralists in Africa and of the Cheyenne Indians (right). Other traditions preferred the stark geometry of the chess board for organizing cities. The Chinese during the Shang dynasty codified the perfect square as the ideal layout. In societies such as these, which relied on religious order and social control, straight lines were meant to sustain harmony and came to dominate the layout of cities, from Chang'an in China to Teotihuacan in Ancient Mexico to present-day New York.

Camp circle
The Cheyenne Indians erected tents, making huge camp circles, which were compared to the stars.

Zulu circle
Zulu cattle herders live in semi-permanent villages. Cattle represent wealth and are kept in the centre kraal at night.

Medieval city
Most medieval cities were fortified by ring walls.

Bursting out
The sprawl of modern cities bursts into the country.

The crossed circle
The symbol of the crossed circle (below) is a layout for settlements that recurs in many cultures. Cross-roads were the central growth points of many an emergent city, usually marked by a holy building – the spiritual hub of the urban cosmos. The Ancient Egyptians used the circle, crossed into four segments, as their hieroglyph symbolizing town, or city.

"Come let us make bricks and bake them hard. Come, let us build ourselves a city and a tower with its top in the heavens, and make a name for ourselves; or we shall be dispersed all over the world."

Genesis 11, 3-5

(see pp. 44-5). Many were "free cities" under the control of the citizens rather than of the feudal overlords. The subsequent age of the Renaissance put the aristocracy back in charge, supported by new military technology. It also reinstated ancient ideas of urban grandeur (see pp. 46-7). Cities such as Florence profit from their sheer magnificence to this very day.

Modern times

Since the 18th century Europe and North America have experienced an urban boom as a result of the Industrial Revolution and global trade. Ever since that time efforts have been made to counter unplanned and disorderly urban sprawl with coherent planning concepts, to turn settlements into "orderly" places. But all over the world cities have tended to defy rational planners, sometimes spreading uncontrollably, driven by the motor of industrial growth. Today, with megacities feeding off a global hinterland, new popular ideas are required to ensure the sustainability of our cities.

Ancient cities

No one is certain why the very first cities came into being but farming and trade were important factors. Six thousand years ago several towns sprang up in the fertile river delta of Mesopotamia. This area had been farmed for centuries, and with its hot climate could produce several harvests a year. The plains were surrounded by forested slopes, to which wheat and barley were native. The two major rivers, the Tigris and the Euphrates, flowed down from these hills, but they had the habit of flooding the plains, making it necessary to control their flow and moods. The inhabitants of Mesopotamia were forced to develop elaborate systems of co-operation to gain the greatest benefit from their rich, yet difficult, environment and control the rivers. Flood control and irrigation were vital for the farmers who cultivated this land where rain was rare.

Farming was successful, and large agricultural surpluses led to a diversification of trades and increased division of labour, eventually producing a highly stratified society. The well established social stratification of these cities is recorded by the greatly differing wealth contained in excavated tombs. Villages and small towns grew into cities. By 4000BC the population explosion in Mesopotamia was in

Cities of Sumeria: victims of salt
Ancient clay tablets recorded the changing yields of different grains being grown in Sumer or Mesopotamia. Wheat was the most popular crop, but gradually wheat crops started to fail. This was because the Sumerians did not use drainage ditches to remove surplus water from the irrigated land and with the evaporation of the slightly salty irrigation water from the fields, the soil consequently became salt-laden. Farmers were forced to grow barley instead, which is more salt-tolerant. But the soil became ever-saltier and even barley proved too difficult to grow.

Today the Ancient cities of Sumeria are a windswept wasteland and modern Iraq has inherited the salty soils. The state spends vast sums of oil money trying to wash the salt out of the soil – and has to import 70% of its food. The mistakes of the Sumerians are being repeated in many parts of the world today, since farmers still fail to dig drainage ditches on irrigated land to prevent salination.

full swing. By 3500BC there were many prosperous walled cities dotted on the landscape of the lower Tigris-Euphrates basin, each surrounded by irrigated fields and villages.

The Ancient cities of the near East all share a number of key features. They were administered by male priests, initially serving a female deity. They were permeated with fields, with most citizens farming part-time. Soon each city was organized as a self-contained state. "Ensi", priest-kings, ruled their cities with the advice of a council of elders. As the cities grew, typically to between 10,000 and 30,000 people, they acquired imposing ceremonial structures – ziggurats and temples. Male gods increasingly replaced the former female ones. The temples were surrounded by administrative buildings, workshops, dwellings, and finally, by walls topped with watch towers. Never before had man had the power to impose huge structures of stone on an "innocent" landscape.

Mesopotamia was not the only centre of Ancient urban growth. Other river valleys, too, such as the Nile, the Indus, and the Hwang Ho were centres of early civilization. The Negev in Palestine spawned cities as soon as the technology for drilling wells was mastered. All these urban centres appear to have traded precious objects, as well as ideas, with each other, such as the use of the plough, of metals, of draught animals, and of the art of writing.

Ur: victim of floods

The Ancient city of Ur, which probably accommodated around 50,000 people, was excavated by the archaeologist Sir Leonard Woolley. Having dug through a metre of soil littered with potsherds and other human artefacts, he found a three-metre layer of virgin soil and then, below that, more traces of human activity. Could this virgin soil be a relic of Noah's flood? There is no doubt that the thick layer of mud found at Ur and subsequently at other Mesopotamian cities was the result of massive flooding and soil erosion originating from the hills that border the plains of Mesopotamia. The appetite of the ancient cities for timber and farmland had denuded the hills and caused the first man-made environmental disaster.

Decline and fall

Cities indicate an anxious quest for permanence transcending the inevitability of human mortality. Yet this quest is laced with a large dose of hubris. The sheer magnificence of the cities of Mesopotamia led to inequality and jealousies within and between the city states. There appears to have been a permanent state of war between city states vying for each other's wealth. And every so often bands of invaders would descend from the Taurus or the Zagros mountains to try to ransack a city. Only ruins are left of such attempts to impose permanence and immortality.

Uruk, Ur, Nineveh, and Babylon were no more than mythological names in the Old Testament until the present century, when excavations led to the discovery of ancient ruins confirming the actual historical existence of these cities. None has survived as a living city today.

Wasted hinterlands

Many cities in history literally "ate" their hinterlands, ultimately causing their own demise. Urbanization invariably means the concentration of large numbers of people in a small area whose needs have to be supplied from outside: much of the water, food, timber, and fuel has to be imported. Many Ancient cities took the natural wealth of their hinterland without concern for replenishing it. Soil fertility was depleted as food was taken from the country to the city, and the plant nutrients were never replaced. This one-way traffic of natural products to the city is the main cause for the inherent environmental instability of cities.

Rome's hinterland

Rome was Europe's greatest Ancient city, accommodating a million people by AD100. The Romans neglected their own local agriculture, which would have fed Rome quite comfortably, if properly cultivated. The city, however, was forced to import food from across its empire, which Julius Caesar had extended to include most of Africa north of the Sahara. Caesar's war veterans settled the land there, cleared the forests and began to farm the land; up to 500,000 tonnes of grain were shipped from Africa to Rome each year.

The rise and fall of Teotihuacan

The great city of Teotihuacan was at its peak by AD450, with a population of 140,000 people, and was an important commercial and trade centre. It was located on a rich alluvial plain, ideal for irrigated agriculture, but the valley was small and food had to be brought in from further afield and exchanged for trade goods such as obsidian. Obsidian was valued for its hard cutting edge and there were large deposits locally. After AD500 the city declined, mainly because supplies of obsidian ran out. Ironically the obsidian axes, which had made the city so wealthy, contributed to deforestation of local hillsides. Deforestation increased aridity and soil erosion, and soil moisture was lost, making farming difficult. Finally, around AD750, the city was looted and burned, signalling its end.

Rome reaches out

Rome was the zenith of Ancient European civilization, but it achieved this status at a price. It had to reach out further and further to supply itself with grain. Eventually the supply lines became overstretched and Rome collapsed, in part because of environmental decline: loss of soil fertility and

Animals
The forests of Algeria and Morocco were ransacked for lions, leopards, panthers, and bears to supply the amphitheatres.

Timber
Forests were cut down both to supply fuel and timber and to clear land for farming. The rare woods of north Africa were much sought after by Roman plutocrats. Cicero paid the equivalent of thousands of pounds for a thuya-wood table top carved in one piece.

deforestation. The fertility of north Africa was shovelled through Roman digestive systems, and then flushed into the Mediterranean, never to be returned to the land. By AD600 many cities of the empire had collapsed and today most of the 600 Roman cities of north Africa, such as Leptis Magna, are piles of rubble in a denuded landscape.

". . . the world is growing old and does not remain in its former vigour. The rainfall and the sun's warmth are both diminishing; the metals are nearly exhausted; the husbandsman is failing in his field . . . springs which once gushed forth liberally, now barely give a trickle of water."

St Cyprian, Bishop of Carthage, AD250

Olives
Olive oil, harvested from African olive trees, was a most valued commodity in Rome.

Grain
By 50BC, Africa produced 500,000 tonnes of grain per year. A century later it provided two-thirds of Rome's wheat needs.

Ivory, stone, and marble
The elephant was hunted for its tusks until it was eradicated from the area. Quarries provided stone and marble for use as tesserae in mosaics.

Slaves
Thousands of African hunter-gatherers and nomads were enslaved in Roman workshops, quarries, households, and warships.

Rome collapses

In AD455 Gaiseric the Vandal looted Rome from his base in north Africa, and withheld vital north African grain supplies from Rome. The great city never recovered its power and other cities of the empire also collapsed. Long-distance trade was reduced to a trickle. The "Dark Ages" saw much of Europe return to an agricultural subsistence economy.

Iron technology had a major impact on life in the Middle Ages. Iron swords and lances turned horsemen clad in metal armour into fearsome warriors. Stirrups, introduced from China, fused the knights to their iron-shod horses. Iron ploughs pulled by horses increased the land's agricultural productivity. Better crop rotations, windmills, and watermills, with their many uses, all helped lay the economic foundations for a new prosperity.

Urbanization in full swing

The new rural technologies released many labourers from the land. They flocked to the new "free cities" of Europe that were controlled by citizens, not feudal lords. By AD1200 urbanization was taking hold again right across Europe. The great Gothic cathedrals in the city centres symbolized the new cultural self-confidence of northern Europe. In France alone 80 cathedrals and 500 large churches were built between 1050 and 1350.

Medieval cities: cities for people

Thousands of towns and cities built in the Middle Ages still exist today. For a few hundred years many gained their freedom from taxes imposed by local lords, however every able-bodied person was obliged to contribute to building and safeguarding the city walls. The walls had defensive functions, but they also guaranteed the citizens internal self-determination. The wall symbolized the "free" collaboration of merchants, priests, scholars, craftsmen, and warriors that gave medieval cities their special dynamism.

Medieval towns were, above all, market towns, with traders and producers selling their wares. Long-distance trade also played a major role in many medieval cities. Bruges, for instance, grew

Dinkelsbühl: the closed circle

The complete ring wall of Dinkelsbühl, Germany, from above resembles a stone collar, keeping the town separate from the world outside. The centrepiece of the town is the Gothic cathedral. Crafts guilds made the town prosperous – cloth-making, beer-brewing, tanning, corn-milling, and furniture manufacture. Most of these trades depended on the fertility of the surrounding countryside to supply the raw materials. The land usually belonged to farmers who lived

within the city walls. Even today cows are herded from the fields through the town gates into sheds for the night. Dung heaps are still stacked against the wall and manure is returned to the land. And so the cycle of plant growth, harvest, and decay is closed again and again, making medieval towns sustainable.

Dinkelsbühl today
A town of 11,000 inhabitants largely unchanged since its beginnings 700 years ago. The ring wall (below) is still intact, but today the walls are not manned by archers, but by tourists with their cameras.

rich by weaving wool from Britain. Florence, too, prospered from its woollen industry until banking came to dominate its economy.

Supreme trading cities

Constantinople, by far Europe's largest city and premier trading centre, became the true heir to the Roman legacy during the Middle Ages. Constantinople exchanged the riches of India, Africa, and the Mediterranean basin for woollens and iron products from western Europe.

At the end of the Middle Ages, Venice was western Europe's first city to live and prosper by commerce. Venice was wedded to the sea, trading in spices, silks, ivory, and precious stones and metals from as far afield as Persia, India, and north Africa. Venice had a wealthy economy and the city eventually became a Renaissance centre of learning, art, and music on the basis of its trading wealth.

Renaissance: the birth of humanism

With the fall of its empire Rome had become a shadow of its former self. Its temples had been plundered and its churches ruined. Its famous aqueducts were defunct. But the age of the Renaissance ("rebirth") rose out of its ruins.

The writings of Vitruvius, Ancient Rome's greatest urban theoretician, were rediscovered by the architect Leone Battista Alberti. Alberti initiated the classical city revival to resurrect ancient glory and to counter the Gothic style that had spread from "upstart" northern Europe. By 1453 Alberti had restored one of Rome's aqueducts, bringing water back into the city, and had started to rebuild the city's ruined ancient monuments. Alberti's vision was to give cities a new heart, a great municipal centre with magnificent piazzas to instill pride and a sense of identity in their people. Renaissance cities celebrated the growth of a new urban aristocracy and the architectural magnificence of the cities reflected a new, classically inspired, creativity. Renaissance cities were centres of a humanistic world view in which people, rather than God or nature, took centre stage. This humanist, cultural legacy prospers to this very day.

Aristocratic power and urban magnificence

Before 1500, the Medici family presided over Florence. The Italian urban nobility were powerfully motivated by city pride. Trading wealth was converted into architectural beauty, and art of unrivalled splendour. Cities within Italy, and right across Europe, competed in trying to outdo each other's cultural achievements.

Europe's new imported wealth
After 1500, the wealth of gold and silver robbed by the Spanish from Aztec and Inca cities in South America, brought about economic and urban growth in Europe. Madrid became Spain's elegant new capital. It was the centre of the first new European colonial empire, soon to be followed by Amsterdam, Paris, and London.

Renaissance Florence
Florence (below), the heart of Renaissance Italy, dominated by Brunelleschi's imposing cathedral, a magnificent architectural achievement.

The sun never sets

London – the growth of a world city

Medieval London, like all pre-industrial cities, relied for its food and fuel supply on its immediate hinterland. Food came mainly from the Home Counties, only Kent supplying the grain and Suffolk the dairy produce. As the city consolidated its hold on the British Isles, its increasing demands were met by supplies from further afield. Drovers herded their cattle and sheep from Wales and Scotland, and from the 16th century, the major bulk of fuel was transported as "sea coal" on freighters from northern England. From the beginning of the 18th century grain was increasingly imported from abroad.

Up until 1700 London's power and population compared with other European capitals, but from the 18th century onward Britain's colonial trade, backed by its naval power, outstripped that of all other European states. With the development of steam engines, Britain had a technological lead that contributed to its economic and urban growth. By 1800 London was Europe's largest city.

London's port trade

The conquest of overseas territories led to an enormous increase in shipping-related employment. A quarter of London's population already lived off the port trade in 1700, and for hundreds of years after that London had a major ship-building and maintenance industry. By the 1820s London had the world's largest warehousing system, with a port capable of accommodating 1400 merchant vessels.

London never became Britain's leading industrial centre, but trade, conducted by private companies, spawned local industries to handle and process precious goods. There was therefore plenty of productive employment for artisans such as silk-weavers, tailors, shoemakers, printers, bookbinders, bakers, brewers, gin manufacturers, watch- and clock-makers, potters, jewellers, soap, glass, and furniture-makers. The financial return on trade was massive, and consequently the City of London became the world's financial capital. By 1861, 29,000 people worked in the city and by 1914 London had invested about £4000 million overseas.

As metropolitan London expanded, it needed new colonial cities from which to control the empire. It was like a giant spider at the nerve centre of a vastly complex web of trade links – a new type of world economy. Some sixty colonial cities became the administrative, military, and trade centres through which the British empire was managed. A few thousand expatriates governed the lives of a vast subject population.

Calcutta: dream and nightmare
Calcutta was created by the East India Trading Company, which needed a base with good access to the rich trade of the Ganges valley. The site was the furthest inland point that ocean-going ships could reach. A huddle of villages until 1656, Calcutta grew into India's largest city (11,800,000 people in 1990). The terrain was swampy and mosquito-infested, but traders could make fortunes from trading jute, raw cotton, rice, tea, spices, silks, and precious stones for woven cotton, woollens, machinery, ships, table and ironware. By 1800 Calcutta had a population of 200,000 and by 1948 this number had grown to 1.4 million.

The growth of London and the British empire
The growth in population of London (and corresponding growth in area) in the 17th, 18th, and 19th centuries (see right) parallels the expansion of the British empire and the development of colonial cities.

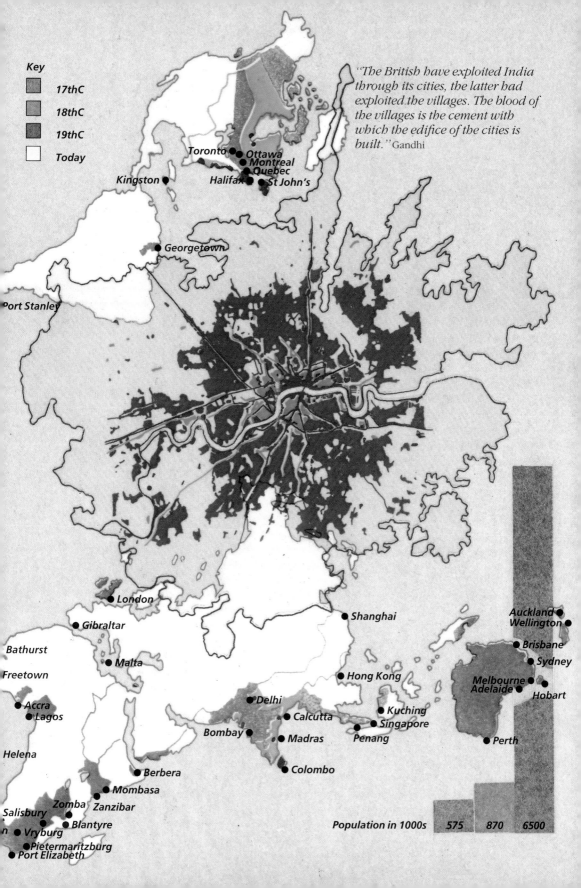

Key

- 17thC
- 18thC
- 19thC
- Today

"The British have exploited India through its cities, the latter had exploited the villages. The blood of the villages is the cement with which the edifice of the cities is built." Gandhi

Toronto
Ottawa
Montreal
Quebec
Kingston
Halifax
St John's

Georgetown

Port Stanley

London

Gibraltar

Bathurst

Malta

Freetown

Accra
Lagos

Helena

Berbera

Mombasa

Zomba
Zanzibar

Salisbury

Blantyre

Vryburg

Pietermaritzburg
Port Elizabeth

Shanghai

Auckland
Wellington

Brisbane
Sydney

Hong Kong

Melbourne
Adelaide
Hobart

Delhi

Calcutta

Kuching

Bombay

Singapore
Penang

Madras

Perth

Colombo

Population in 1000s   575   870   6500

The power of king coal

In the Black Country

Long-distance trade and coal mining were two major factors that changed the world, and turned 18th-century Britain from a rural society into an urban one. In the 17th century coal began to attract much investment and coal mining areas soon became the sites for new industrial cities. Industrial production became the motor of urban growth and as London burst its seams, so too did the cities of central and northern Britain. Industrial cities such as Newcastle, Birmingham, Leeds, and Manchester became the British counterparts of colonial centres such as Calcutta, Sydney, Lagos, Mombassa and Montreal (see pp. 48-9).

Industrial squalor

Monumental factories sprang up everywhere to house the huge stationary engines and machines. The new urban "working classes" were relegated to the role of machine minders. As factories grew, so did "those separate territories, assigned to poverty" (Engels). In Liverpool in the 1880s population density reached 3000 people per hectare – people lived anywhere they could, even cellars were packed full. The new cities were blanketed with acrid smoke, and they became breeding grounds for bronchitis and tuberculosis: they were "manheaps, machine warrens, not organs of human association" (Lewis Mumford), and yet the people kept coming.

Monster conurbations

Once steam engines were no longer stationary, but able to power locomotives and ships, they became the real force behind the growth of the cities of capitalism and colonialism. This happened first in 19th-century Britain, closely followed by Belgium and Germany. The Ruhr area in Germany became the second largest centre for coal and iron industries after Britain's Black Country. Provincial German towns grew into vast conurbations and urban growth was phenomenal; the Ruhr population increased from 237,000 people in 1843 to 1.5 million in 1895. Ruhr towns such as Essen, Gelsenkirchen, and Bochum filled up with miners, some migrating from as far as Poland and Czechoslovakia.

By the 17th century Britain's economy had outgrown its resources of timber, firewood, and charcoal; coal came to the rescue. Coal production in Britain rose from three million tonnes in 1700 to ten million tonnes by 1800.

In the 1730s as soon as methods of turning coal into coke for making pig iron were perfected, there was no limit to Britain's iron- and steel-producing capacity. The steam engine designed 40 years later by James Watt was crucial for a further expansion in coal production. Watt's engines were perfect for pumping water out of coal mines. Thus steam technology assured a supply of coal, the very fuel that guaranteed the further expansion of its use. But where there is fire there is smoke, and coal smoke soon began to damage the forests that had been rescued by substituting coal for firewood.

". . . the vaporous poison of their ovens and chimneys has soiled and shrivelled the surrounding country till there is no village lane within a league but what offers a gaunt and ludicrous travesty of rural charms. . .. the subsidiary industries of coal and iron prosper amid a wreck of verdure, the struggle is grim, appalling, heroic – so ruthless is [man's] havoc of [nature], so indomitable her ceaseless recuperation."

Arnold Bennett, *Anna of the Five Towns,* 1902

The industrial scene
A view of Sheffield, England (above)
and the interior of a 19th-century
pottery in Lambeth, London
(below).

*"...tall chimneys...poured out their
plague of smoke, obscured the light, and
made foul the melancholy air."*

Charles Dickens, *The Old Curiosity Shop*, 1841

Imposing magnificence

Paris: people versus monarch

Throughout history city people have confronted rulers and their "unjust" laws and taxes. Nowhere more so than in Paris; in its 2000-year history popular rebellions alternated with autocratic rule. In 1789 the independent-spirited people of Paris, by then a city of 600,000 people, took the lead in the revolution to overthrow the *ancien régime*. Thousands of noblemen were guillotined as Parisians cheered. But in 1804 the peoples' revolution gave way to a new monarch as the power of the people was usurped by Emperor Napoleon I. His eventual successor, Napoleon III, wanted a capital worthy of a great imperial power, free from hiding places for anarchists, and fit for a modern society. City prefect Baron Haussmann was charged with rebuilding the city; he started by cutting through the maze of medieval streets and eventually built grand boulevards. They were designed to maximize the show of splendour and power of the great imperial city and its army and to improve riot and crowd control.

In 1870-1 the Parisians tried once more to control their destiny, but the "Paris Commune" was short-lived. A new, international world was opening up and Paris was teeming with foreign visitors. In 1889 the Eiffel Tower, standing at 300m, became Paris's new symbol of greatness.

Haussmannization and Europe's great capitals

The reshaping of Paris by Haussmann was widely noted by city planners all over Europe. Vienna, was surrounded by defensive walls, which by the mid-1900s were perceived to be obsolete. They were levelled to make space for the Ringstrasse, a boulevard around the inner city, along which great museums and administrative buildings were set in spacious grounds. Thus Vienna gave itself a facelift to match the grandeur of Haussmann's Paris.

Berlin grew in the 19th century from 200,000 to over 2,000,000 people, and it became an imperial capital. Despite this explosive growth the city authorities made sure of a generous layout for the centre, appropriate for the capital of the new, unified Germany. Wide avenues were built, suitable for grand military parades.

In the mid-17th century Louis XIV decided to put his mark on Paris. He began adorning medieval Paris with magnificent new buildings, such as the Louvre.

It was Napoleon III who 150 years later imposed the rule of the straight line on the city. He decided to scrap much of what was left of medieval Paris; many old houses, built along meandering streets, were destroyed to make way for straight avenues. Haussmann constructed 100km of magnificent, gas-lit boulevards that could be controlled by the fire power of the army. He also modernized the city's services, building a modern pumped water supply, and a sewage system. These were followed by market halls, an opera house, and English-style parks. The magnificent new city was a grand gesture of urban planning, and Paris became a city ready to welcome visitors, who soon flocked in from around the world.

Paris feeding itself
Paris has long been surrounded by market gardens. In the late 1800s the Russian urbanist Kropotkin was impressed by their productivity, achieved by recycling and composting human and animal wastes. Irrigation, heated beds, and glass houses achieved huge yields on 860 hectares worked by 5000 people. They supplied the 2 million Parisians with fruit and vegetables; excess produce was sold to London.

Paris: the elegant capital
Haussmann's splendid boulevards (right) radiate from the Arc de Triomphe.

The city in the garden

The marriage of town and country

At the turn of the 20th century London became the world's largest city. It was a place of economic opportunity, but also of congestion, squalor, and pollution. Ebenezer Howard sought to solve the problems of the congested city and the "undeveloped" countryside in one fell swoop. His aim was to achieve a marriage between town and country, merging the benefits of both in one place.

Howard wanted people from overcrowded city centres to move into his new "Garden Cities", leaving space for improving the city centre. He envisaged Garden Cities as being moderately sized, self-contained, and capable of all the functions of an urban community. They would have their own employment opportunities and would be surrounded by a farm belt, to be farmed on behalf of the community. The green belt would provide food and also serve as a barrier to limit urban sprawl. Howard literally envisaged "planting" his cities in a "host landscape". A "city in the garden", with full employment, social, and cultural facilities would lead to harmony between people, and also between human beings and nature. Howard planned towns in a leafy, airy, and healthy environment. His purpose was to enable people to live healthily in a diverse landscape.

The co-operative city

Howard was interested in more than just the physical plans of a city, he was a strong believer in shared ownership of land. He proposed the purchase of land at low, agricultural values and that all houses and factories should be leaseholds, rent being used to repay the investors. Eventually any increase in land values would accrue to the whole community. Excess money from rent would then be used to set up pension funds and community services. Howard wanted the Garden City to be socially, economically, as well as ecologically, sustainable.

Although Howard's ideas were influential, only two real Garden Cities were built in Britain, Letchworth and Welwyn Garden City. Other developments, such as Hampstead Garden Suburb, turned into blends of garden city and conventional suburb.

Dreaming of garden cities was not enough for Howard. After publishing his book *Garden Cities of Tomorrow* in 1898, a site in Hertfordshire was purchased to build Letchworth, Britain's first Garden City.

Howard's ideas received worldwide acclaim. In Germany the strongest response came from the steel company Krupp, concerned about the "low morals" of badly housed workers. Krupp built a garden village, Margarethenhöhe, on the edge of Essen. In the USA however, the developments that were built – such as Sunnyside Gardens near New York, Chatham Village in Pittsburgh, and Radburn, New Jersey, which was pioneered by Clarence Stein – ended up as leafy suburbs rather than true Garden Cities.

"Town and country must be married, and out of the joyous union will spring a new hope, a new life, a new civilization"

Fischer, 1976

Welwyn Garden City today
Welwyn in Hertfordshire (right) was Howard's second Garden City, designed in neo-Georgian style. Now a city of 100,000 people, it is a Garden City in form, but not in function: it is within the commuter belt of London, and its agricultural belt never became a reality.

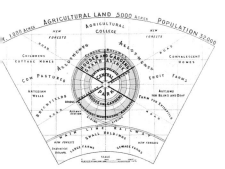

Garden City: theory and practice
*Howard's cities were to house
32,000 people with no more than 30
houses per hectare. Central parkland was to be surrounded by housing, and the factories were to be on
the outskirts, all enclosed by the
city's green belt. Howard wanted
sewage to be recycled back to the
land. His cities were to be independent, not satellite towns to the capital city. In 1919 Howard started his
second project, Welwyn Garden
City. As the map (right) shows reality
differs radically from abstract theor-
etical diagrams (above).*

A new age, a new architecture

After World War I a school of planning and architecture was born in France and Germany that proposed very different solutions to Howard's Garden Cities (see pp. 54-5). Le Corbusier, in France, and Mies van der Rohe and Walter Gropius at the "Bauhaus" in Germany had new ideas about planning cities. The spirit of the age was all about making a fresh start and creating a "new man". This was reflected in radical new approaches to architecture, planning, and housing people.

Le Corbusier was the most vocal guru of "modernism", advocating large, angular building shapes. He proposed housing hundreds, even thousands, of people under one flat roof. He cherished new construction technology; concrete, iron girders, and plate glass were considered preferable to brick, timber, and leaded windows. Le Corbusier praised the totalitarian approach to city planning that had been adopted by Napoleon and Haussmann (see pp. 52-3). Le Corbusier also believed that pure geometry was the solution to planning cities and buildings. He called for the rule of the right angle and the straight line; there was no room for nostalgia and traditional, vernacular shapes. After all, this was the age of the machine and Le Corbusier believed houses were "machines for living in". His proposed blocks had nothing personal and intimate about them; apartments to him were "cells".

Le Corbusier's goals

Like Howard, Le Corbusier also used the term "Garden City", but the gardens of his city were far from being quaint cottage gardens with roses and rows of cabbages. His concept was of a decongested city with large blocks of flats towering over open, tree-dotted space. People from the flats could only see the crowns of trees in the park-like landscape below. His tamed natural world was designed to be visual rather than palpable. Le Corbusier emphasized his preference for geometry and industry over nature. In 1925 he went so far as to praise the fact that cities were an assault on nature. It took 20 years, and the destruction of World War II, for his ideas to come into their own.

Cities against nature

Le Corbusier planned only one real city, Chandigarh, a new capital for India's Punjab. He designed it as an American or European city, suitable for the routine use of cars. Chandigarh's spacial arrangement is for a machine age, not for the traditional, intimate Indian way of life.

Brasilia, another brave new capital, even though not designed by Le Corbusier, owes much to him. Its layout, as he envisaged, allows for free circulation of traffic and open spaces, but it offers no intimacy and lacks a centre.

Architects "know best"

Le Corbusier will always be remembered for the concept of houses as "machines for living in". His sense of angular orderliness has shaped the cities of our time, and it corresponded with the new industrialized building technologies. His blocks were partly conceived as space-saving buildings which would leave room for green spaces in garden cities. But, he never asked people how they really wanted to live. Many architects continue to work under the influence of the master and his contemporaries. Time will tell what the final verdict will be.

"Machinery is the result of geometry. The age in which we live is therefore essentially a geometric one. . . . The result of true geometry is repetition. The result of repetition is a standard, the perfect form."

Le Corbusier

Machines for living in

Le Corbusier (below) holding a model of his "unité d'habitation". He was only able to build this, his master plan, once in Marseilles. But his followers have since built thousands of similar high-rise blocks all over the world.

Brave new Milton Keynes

Moving out – the land beyond the smoke

In the first half of the 20th century the response to city overcrowding in Britain was to encourage suburb growth. Transport technology made this possible and cities sprawled out into the country along rail and commuter lines. From 1900 to 1950 in Britain, 10 million people moved into suburbs, compared with only 40,000 who moved into Howard's Garden Cities (see pp. 54-5). Rural England was under threat, and ways had to be found to contain urban sprawl.

The Greater London Plan

After World War II the government decided that only bold initiatives could solve the housing problems of Britain's cities. The Greater London Plan drawn up by Patrick Abercrombie proposed that London's growth should be confined within a green belt in a radius of 40km around the city centre. The plan, a model for megacities all over the world today, was later complemented by the 1947 New Towns Act.

Post-war New Towns

By 1950 work on 13 New Towns was under way to relieve the overcrowding of London, Birmingham, Liverpool, Manchester, and Glasgow. Many ideas were borrowed from Howard, though the state funded the building, not co-operative companies. The concept of the green belt was adhered to, but it was not the farm belt, fertilized by sewage, that Howard envisaged, it was a "green girdle" of parkland suitable for picnics. By the early 1970s no less than 25 New Towns had been constructed in Britain, housing 1,300,000 people.

Britain's New Towns were built in direct response to the problems of massive growth in cities as a result of the Industrial Revolution and the colonial era. Britain became a mecca for planners from all over the world. But only the former Soviet Union had a New Town programme on the same scale as Britain's. Other countries built New Towns on the outskirts of existing ones, for example Vallingby in Sweden was built as a satellite town for Stockholm. In Australia Canberra was built as a New Town.

Milton Keynes in Buckinghamshire is Britain's largest New Town. Built on 8800 hectares, the new city is close to its projected population of 250,000 people. It has attracted enough companies to make it an economic success. Most housing is owner-occupied on village-like estates, some of which feature energy-efficient designs. Millions of trees have been planted, which make parts of Milton Keynes look like a city in a forest, but the low-density lay-out makes the use of cars

a necessity. Milton Keynes is, however, still without a cultural centre, and has yet to mature into a "real" city with the variety of facilities expected for a city of this size.

The bomb and the bulldozer

War damage and slum clearance

World War II took a heavy toll on cities and city people. Bomb damage in London, Berlin, Coventry, Bristol, Rotterdam, Leipzig, Duisburg, Dresden, and many other great cities was widespread, in some instances destroying over 50 per cent of the city. On 6 August 1945 Hiroshima became the world's first radioactive wasteland. As the war ended, the bulldozer took over from the bombs. Some planners saw this as an opportunity for slum clearance and so were not sorry to see "outdated" brick-built terraces demolished. New construction methods were called for as an unprecedented building boom commenced: the age of the kit-built concrete-panel tower block had arrived and in Britain alone 384 housing blocks were built between 1964 and 1974.

The building boom

The new municipal styles of architecture were similar in capitalist and socialist countries. In the former Eastern bloc countries high-rise towers became synonymous with socialist development; the "ideal" unit of collective housing. In the former Soviet Union alone well over 100 new towns were built consisting almost entirely of such towers, while in Germany baroque cities such as Dresden, smashed by allied bombs, rose out of the ashes of war as angular structures last seen in Le Corbusier's design handbooks. In Romania, "outdated" villages were removed and replaced with concrete tower blocks.

High-rise life

Quite apart from the lack of individuality, "soul", and the sheer ugliness of such buildings, tower blocks quickly proved to be difficult to live in (see pp. 80-3). Eventually, in the late 1960s and early 1970s the structural problems associated with these towers and their unpopularity, highlighted by the collapse of Ronan Point in London in 1968, led to major changes in housing policy. It became apparent that lack of consultation with people about their housing needs and preferences was a huge error, added to which few architects had ever actually lived in any of the high-rise housing developments that had come off their own drawing boards.

All over Europe and as far afield as South America and South Korea the new blocks went up, made of pre-fabricated concrete panels mounted on steel skeletons. The crane had taken over from the trowel as the main building tool and bulldozers were in demand as never before. Even where there had been no war damage, rows of terraced houses were cleared to make way for the highrise blocks. It was not only war damage and the new building technologies that gave birth to this but also the "triumph of newness" in the face of which quaint old buildings seemed undesirable.

"The first mistake was the overvaluation of mechanization and standardization as ends in themselves without respect to human purpose. . . .This is the error of the disposable urban container."

Lewis Mumford on Le Corbusier

Out with the old, in with the new
The machine (below) that destroyed the old and erected the new was controlled by a mindset determined to eradicate the past and replace it with the "modern", the "clean", and the "new".

Shrinking distance

In the United States in the 1930s Frank Lloyd Wright developed planning concepts that were highly influential. He described his vision, "Broadacre City", in his book *The Disappearing City*. The city centre would be each family's own home and traditional civic centres – schools, museums, galleries, swimming pools, zoological and botanical gardens – would be replaced by activity nodes spread throughout the sprawling city. Cars would shrink distances like no other mode of transport: running on a dense network of highways they would free people from the inflexibility of rail travel.

Self-determining families

Wright proposed that each house should be set in about an acre of land, so that families could grow their own food. He believed that everyone should have the freedom to be part farmer, artist, businessperson, or factory worker, and to determine their own lives. There is a strong element of traditional American homesteading in Wright's proposals, but his vision also drew on the experiences of the Depression of the 1930s, when people had become weary of the uncertainties of depending on industrial or commercial employment.

The adjusting landscape

Wright's vision anticipated the implications of major advances. People have learned to use time rather than distance as a measure of their mobility: it is the landscape around them that has had to adjust. The freeway has come to rule the landscape of the United States and now of Europe, too. With transport technology as both master and servant, nature and tradition have fallen by the wayside.

Great visions

Some aspects of Wright's thinking are similar to Howard's (see pp. 54-5). For example, Wright envisaged much of Broadacre City to be taken up by productive farms, but Wright's concept is based on the self-determination of the individual rather than Howard's co-operative model. The spaciousness of

From Broadacre to crystal city

Wright believed fervently in the freedom of the individual and to his mind the best way to achieve this was for each person to own a plot of land: self-determination could be achieved by the spacious layout of his Broadacre City. Post-war urban America is Broadacre City, minus the farms. Urban sprawl has become the rule as millions of people now have their plot of land, but few grow food on it as Wright imagined. The space around the house is leisure land; trimmed grass not potato patch. And neither has the city centre gone. Every American city has a collection of giant crystals – office blocks that house oil companies, hi-tech corporations, or banks. Los Angeles, Dallas, Phoenix, and Atlanta all identify their financial muscle with the size of their skyscrapers.

"It is significant that not only have space values entirely changed to time values, now ready to form new standards of movement-measurement but a new sense of spacing based upon speed is here."

Frank Lloyd Wright

"The towers were jammed together so tightly, he could feel the mass and stupendous weight. . . . There it was, the Rome, the Paris, the London of the twentieth century, the city [Manhattan] of ambition, the dense magnetic rock, the irresistible destination of all those who insist on being where things are happening . . ."

Tom Wolfe, *The Bonfire of the Vanities*, 1987

Skyscrapers
Symbols of monetary might, skyscrapers represent a total commitment to technology as well as access to virtually unlimited amounts of energy. They can exist only because of a vast industrial infrastructure that urban capital has helped to create.

Horizontal versus vertical
Frank Lloyd Wright's spacious layout (below) relied on personal transport (including helicopters) to shrink distances. In city centres such as the Shinjuku business district in Tokyo (left) companies compete for space and ostentatious towers must grow upward.

Wright's layout resulted in problems similar to those generated by Le Corbusier: isolation of people (see pp. 56-7). All three ideals share the problem of many great visions: they are removed from reality and do not recognize the fact that reality is made by people, and by environmental, economic, and political forces.

The new skyline

The city centre has not disappeared as Wright envisaged, but has grown into collections of high-rise shining towers which now dominate downtown skylines worldwide. Central urban locations are in great demand for business premises, and skyscrapers are a response to high land values in cities where one hectare of land can be worth many millions of dollars. The 1980s post-modern skyscraper, decked out with marble, tropical hardwood veneers, and stainless steel and brass finishes, is an ostentatious expression of wealth and power.

The arrival of megacities

Sometime between World War I and II New York became the first city with 10 million people; the world's first "megacity". At that time London was the only city to approach New York's size. However today, New York has long been overtaken by cities such as Tokyo, which is nearing the 30 million mark, and Mexico City, which is nearing 20 million. New York took 150 years to reach eight million people whereas Mexico City and São Paulo are taking only 15 years to increase their populations *by* eight million.

The new worldwide trend

Urban growth, a trend that started in Europe and America, is now gripping the world and today, for the first time, it is centred on developing countries. Between 1950 and 2000 some 1.4 billion people will have become city dwellers in the developing world. This phenomenal urban growth symbolises the aspirations for financial and economic power of their elites and the determination of their populations, against all the odds, to develop "urban" living standards. Can the planet afford such a determined demand for urban living?

The demands of megacities

As countries are dominated by one or two very large cities, life there is determined by their needs, and the decisions that are made there. Mass communication ensures that culture and people's values become urbanized and the hinterland of such cities tends to become a mere colony.

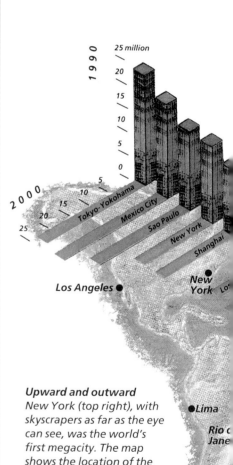

Upward and outward
New York (top right), with skyscrapers as far as the eye can see, was the world's first megacity. The map shows the location of the world's largest cities. The chart compares city populations in 1990 to those predicted for the year 2000.

PART TWO

Sick cities, sick world

The developed countries have taught the world about urban growth. Today the cities of the developing world are outdoing their "teachers", with more pollution and more human misery. They top the urban growth league, but migrants to cities often lack even the most basic housing. Soon peasant-turned-urban dwellers undergo a transformation in values, rapidly becoming thoughtless consumers like all the other city dwellers. The inherent selfishness of modern city-living makes urban growth a global cause for concern. Cities are giant abusers of Gaia and they have little awareness of the consequences of exploiting her.

"The more complete the urbanisation, the more definite is the release from natural limitations; the more highly the city seems developed as an independent entity, the more fatal are the consequences for the territory it dominates."

Lewis Mumford

"No one has driven at snail's pace through London, already late for an appointment and with no guarantee of a parking place at journey's end, without fulminating at the road system; no one has approached Caracas or Rio through the awfulness of their shanty towns without wondering why they are tolerated; or seen the street-sleepers in Calcutta – or those under Charing Cross Bridge, for that matter – without being convinced that man has made his own hell."

Emrys Jones, *Metropolis: the World's Great Cities*

CHAPTER 3
The expanding city

In the grip of urbanization

A great migration is under way. Some 20 million people move to cities every year, a human trans-migration unprecedented in history. From 1950 to 1990 the population of the world's cities went up from 200 million to over two billion, with three billion people expected by 2025. Today there are 20 "megacities" of over 10 million people, and 19 out of the world's 25 largest cities are in developing countries. Worldwide 60 cities have now grown to over four million people.

What is the cause of this astonishing "mobil-ization" of people? Urbanization based on industrial development, a trend that started in Europe and North America is now gripping the world. Tokyo-Yokohama, Hong Kong, Seoul, Mexico City, São Paulo, and many other cities have experienced phenomenal urban, as well as industrial, growth.

In developing countries industrial growth offers employment and trading opportunities for rural people faced with declining living standards due to lack of land, depleted rural environments, or indus-trialization of agriculture. But increasingly urban-ization is occurring without any significant opportunities for migrants. Africa today has the fas-test urban growth anywhere in the world. But many migrants are environmental refugees from badly de-pleted rural areas.

Squatting and highrise living

Newcomers to the city, if they are lucky, have a chance of a little shack in which to live rent free, but usually without even the most elementary services. People tend to try and live close to their source of income, as factory workers, traders, or domestic ser-vants. Urban centres are the preferred locations for the "informal settlements" that permeate develop-ing-world cities. Given half a chance, people will do their best to turn squatter camps into neighbour-hoods to be proud of (see pp. 128-31), using infor-mal patterns of mutual support. But often they are hindered by the authorities who don't like "dis-orderly" camps.

Cities expand outward as the pressure of num-bers dictates urban growth, but they also grow

Urban living standards

In 1990 the Population Crisis Committee in conjunction with 130 urban research institutes worldwide, published a study on the world's 100 largest cities, assessing and group-ing cities according to the living standards they offer. Ten different criteria were used: public safety, food costs, living space, housing standards, communications access, education, public health, peace and quiet, traffic flow, and air quality. Those cities with "very good" living standards, are nearly all in North America, Europe, Australia, or Japan. Cities in the "good" category are mainly in the same area, with the addition of a few eastern European cities. The third category, "fair", consists largely of cities in South America, China, Korea, and North Africa. Those cities with the worst living conditions, "poor", most of which have rapid popu-lation growth but few employment opportunities, are in India, Peru, Brazil, Pakistan, and Africa. Lagos is the lowest-scoring city of all.

The upward spiral
Migrants may be pushed toward cities by failing rural cycles, or pulled by rejection of traditional ways. But unemployment and overcrowding await the hopeful.

Mexico City: opportunity and explosion

Mexico City is a vast industrial and trading centre, with chemical, engineering, and plastics factories, and thousands of small workshops. The country's huge oil resources have brought about the growth of refineries and motor vehicle factories. This activity is responsible for the city's huge in-migration and population growth. Between 1900 and 1990 it rose from 344,000 to 20.2 million. The city increased its share of national production from 29% in 1930 to 45.5% in 1975. By 1983 it was generating 52% of Mexico's industrial production.

*"And they said,
Go to, let us build
us a city and a tower,
whose top may reach
unto heaven;"*

Genesis, 11.iv

upward. Developed and developing-world cities share a post-war architecture that has been called "nissen huts in the sky". In many cities tower blocks have turned into little more than high-rise slums particularly if they are located far away from urban centres with little access to employment. Their design is extraordinarily insensitive to people's real needs to be in close contact with the Earth and each other. Urban stress (see pp. 82-4) is the result of many factors: bad design of buildings and urban environments as well as existential worries and lack of money.

The problems of living in large concrete blocks are particularly acute in cities hit by deindustrialization and unemployment. Many cities in developed countries have suffered the loss of their economic base. Vandalism, gangs, and crime are particularly rife in urban areas that have lost their reason for being.

An urban planet?

In 1925 less than 10 per cent of populations in the developing countries lived in cities. Between 1950 and 1975 the urban areas of these countries absorbed 400 million people. People may move to the city because they are "pushed" by poverty in rural communities or they may be "pulled" by the attractions of city life and the perceived urban opportunities, or they may have followed relatives or friends. Or they may make the move because of a combination of both "push" and "pull" factors. From 1975 to 2000, according to the World Bank, developing-world cities are expected to increase by a further 1000 million. About half of this growth will be accounted for by high reproductive rates of those already living in cities.

Were they "pushed"?

In many parts of the world rural population growth and shortage of good land are the major problems. Forty eight per cent of holdings in developing countries are below one hectare (ha). In Rwanda the size of a typical holding was 1.2 ha, to be divided among several children and eventually, their children. Such circumstances make migration to cities a virtual necessity for farming people.

Land inequality is a key issue in many countries, with small numbers of people owning the bulk of the farmland. Unequal land ownership and the in-

Push factors
- Land degradation
- Lack of adequate land
- Unequal land distribution
- Droughts, storms, floods
- Firewood shortage
- Clean water shortage
- Lack of modern resources
- Pressure of rural population
- Traditional responsibilities
- Religious conflicts
- Local economic decline
- Guerilla and civil war

Pull factors
- Employment opportunities
- Higher incomes
- Urban convenience
- "Bright lights"
- Joining other rural refugees
- Freedom from oppressive lifestyle
- Access to health care
- Education

Land degradation

"Throughout the developing world, land degradation has been the main factor in the migration of subsistence farmers into the slums and shantytowns of major cities, producing desperate populations vulnerable to disease and natural disasters and prone to participate in crime and civil strife. Such exodus from rural to urban areas has exacerbated the already dire urban problems in many developing countries. And, at the same time, it has delayed efforts to rehabilitate and develop rural areas – through the lack of manpower and the increased negligence of the land."

Essam El-Hinnawi, "Environmental Refugees", UNEP, 1985

Macrocephaly
"Macrocephaly", or bigheaded-ness, is the term for the inordinate size of a country's major city given the total population. São Paulo, Mexico City, Caracas, Lima, Tokyo, Manila, Seoul, and Cairo are all examples. Developing-world megacities invariably harbour a major portion of their country's industry, providing employment for millions of people, but depriving smaller cities of an adequate economic base.

Hyper-cities
"The world's "hyper-cities", those with over 15 million people, have reached a size off the scale of human experience. These sprawling, congested urban agglomerations are of an order of magnitude unmatched by any cities in the past. Their management takes us into uncharted territory. At least some experts believe that traditional urban economies of scale are becoming dwarfed by the problem of congestion, that some cities are simply too large to be efficient."

"Cities; Life in the world's 100 largest metropolitan areas", Population Crisis Committee, 1990

dustrialization of farming have caused millions in Latin America to leave the land. Things are made worse by environmental deterioration. In Africa deforestation and droughts are causing farming people to become environmental refugees. Droughts and famines in Ethiopia, for instance, have driven hundreds of thousands of people into squatter camps in Addis Ababa and Cairo.

Changing dynamics
Expanding national and international urban markets for farm produce causes major upheavals in rural economies. Farming areas are drawn within the economic orbit of cities, converting peasant self-sufficiency to cash-cropping. The availability of modern labour-saving farm machinery further reduces rural employment. These changing dynamics of rural-urban relations contribute to an outflow of people with dreams of making good in the city.

Migrants are not always farmers; they may be redundant craftsmen, whose rural workshops have closed due to the growth of industries and trade in cities. As rural crafts production becomes uncompetitive, unemployed artisans are pushed to the cities in search of an income.

Were they pulled?
All over the developing world people succumb to the magnetic pull of urban centres. This is far from irrational – average earnings in the city can be three to four times greater than in the country, though this figure does not include the monetary value of food self-sufficiency that rural people enjoy. Cities, despite their difficulties, seem to offer opportunity. Disease may be a problem, but doctors are easier to find; worldwide the number of children surviving infanthood is significantly higher in cities than in the countryside.

Few are drawn to cities just by the lure of "bright lights" and great expectations, but the excitement of city life and freedom from the constraints of village life are significant "pull" factors.

The harsh reality of urban life
On the surface cities do seem to offer a better life. But for many new urban dwellers the squalor of a squatter camp is an uncertain start. Lack of sanitation, unclean water, air pollution, and poor job prospects are the reality for millions of people.

People storage

The overcrowding problem

Overcrowding is a feature of most major world cities today, but in the cities of the developing world it is a fact of daily life. Lagos tops all other cities with an occupancy rate of 5.8 people per room. By comparison, Indian cities average about 3 people per room, while North American cities have between 0.5 and 1 person per room.

The problem is often extreme in inner cities, largely because it is vital for the urban poor to be as near as possible to any source of work. So migrants gravitate toward city centres and put pressure on any available accommodation there. Tenement blocks and individual dwellings are divided up again and again. In extreme situations, such as in Calcutta, the "hotbed" system provides beds for people on a rotation basis, day and night. Migrants who cannot even afford to rent a bed or the corner of a room end up living on the street or in a squatter camp. Informal settlements built on the urban periphery far away from any employment are often the poorest places, with few chances of improvement. Ironically, however, these crowded conditions also create close-knit mutual support networks.

A place of misery or hope?

In developing-world cities today the illegal occupation of land in squatter or informal settlements is often the only way for people to get a roof over their heads. Every country has its own terms for squatter settlements and they are perceived in ambiguous ways. In Argentina they are known as "villa miserias" translated as townships of misery, in Peru the term "pueblos jovenos" means young community, and in Indonesia "kampung" simply means village.

Flimsy construction on unsuitable land

New squatter dwellings are made from any materials that people can lay their hands on: cardboard, plastic sheeting, plywood, or corrugated iron. The flimsy materials make shacks vulnerable to bad weather, and can pose a serious fire risk. Most squatter settlements lack adequate services; there is no clean water, sanitation, drainage, or electricity.

The post-war "tower-block euphoria" was not only confined to Europe and North America. Developing-world cities also tried to reduce their housing problems by erecting tower blocks and today tens of thousands of blocks dominate their skylines. But storing families in mid-air, with only a window box for growing plants, is the ultimate form of alienation. No wonder self-help, squatter settlements, despite their problems, are in many ways more acceptable. In any case, tower blocks in central locations are usually occupied by middle-class people who can afford servants to make high-rise living more convenient.

"The room had one bed, in which Faustino and his wife slept. The rest of us slept on pieces of cardboard and blankets or rags spread on the floor... That is the way the thirteen of us, five families, arranged ourselves in that little room."

Oscar Lewis, *The Children of Sanchez*, 1961

City densities
Poor cities around the world have extraordinarily high densities of occupation:
(people per room)

- Lagos 5.8
- Guangzhou 5.7
- Johannesburg 5
- Lahore 4.5
- Bombay 4.2
- Jakarta 3.4
- Karachi 3.3
- Bangkok 3.2
- Hyderabad 3.1
- Ho Chi Minh City 3.1
- Bangalore 2.8
- Ahmedabad 2.7
- Algiers 2.5
- Delhi 2.4
- Lima 2.3
- Casablanca 2.3

Filed away
Stacking people in high-rise ''filing cabinets'' may make sense in crowded cities. But living in noisy little boxes in mid-air with nowhere for children to play is many people's vision of hell on Earth.

Worlds apart
Most developing-world urban authorities cannot afford to house people in high rise blocks. Typically, about 50% of their total population live in shanties.

Shanties are often built on areas unfit for human habitation – on rubbish dumps, steep hillsides, areas prone to subsidence or flooding, or on polluted land. In Rio de Janeiro in 1987 hundreds of people died in favelas built on steep slopes when rainstorms washed away the bare soil on which their shacks were built.

The "unsightly" problem

The history of squatter settlements is a story of confrontations: between illegal settlers and governments and urban authorities and private landlords. Authorities tend to consider squatter settlements to be unsightly, and one way of eradicating the "problem" is to bulldoze them. They are often built on land earmarked for development so most developing-world cities have a history of forced evictions. In Seoul, for instance, between 1983 and 1988, over 700,000 people had to give up their often well-built homes to urban redevelopment projects connected with the Olympic Games. Another common practice is to force squatters out of their homes and deposit busloads of people in remote locations. However, given the chance, people drift back to rebuild their homes in the city.

Token development

Throughout the 1960s governments of the developing world initiated projects to provide public housing for the urban poor, using loans from aid agencies or development banks; thousands of concrete towers went up. However, they were really token developments built to impress the voter or the visitor, tending to be made from expensive imported materials, rather than being low-cost, local-style housing. Invariably the construction cost was higher than original estimates, and fewer housing developments were built than planned.

What then is the solution to the developing-world housing problems? Shanties may be a challenge to authority, but they do represent a self-help solution to housing that can benefit city authorities. Squatters have displayed a great deal of resourcefulness, and by housing themselves, provide a low-cost housing option. It is now widely accepted that

Accommodation crush

The accommodation problem of poor cities is well illustrated by the situation in India. By 1981 India's urban population was 156 million, fourth after the United States, the Soviet Union, and China. By the end of the century that population is expected to be the largest in the world – between 350 and 400 million. There will be 20 cities in excess of 1 million people and Calcutta, Bombay, Delhi, and Madras will all

number over 10 million. Even today half the urban population are shanty or slum dwellers. Poverty in the slums, crumbling tenement buildings, means overcrowding, poor sanitation, and risk of disease. But living in urban-fringe shanties, often with few jobs or services, is even more demoralizing. In Bombay some 5 million people are shanty dwellers, and at least 100,000 people live on pavements.

Bombay shanties
Shanty towns permeate most developing-world cities. Located in the close vicinity of the wealthy business district (below), their poverty is a potent reminder of the imbalance of wealth.

upgrading squatter settlements is the only way of solving urban housing problems (see pp. 128-31).

What is absolute poverty?

"A condition of life so limited by malnutrition, illiteracy, disease, squalid surroundings, high infant mortality, and low life expectancy as to be beneath any reasonable definition of human decency." The classic description of absolute poverty, as defined by Robert McNamara, former president of the World Bank, 1978.

Rural beginnings

Rural poverty is one of the main driving forces of urban growth in the developing world (see also pp. 68-71). Major factors are lack of access to suitable farmland, environmental decline, and population growth. The rural poor eke out their living, malnourished, on a never-changing diet of cereals, roots, and legumes. Four-fifths of the world's absolute poor live in the world's two million rural villages. This is where, for most people, the migration to the city starts.

The impact of cities on rural areas is a cause of the decline of traditional communities. Ironically, urban financial power is also the reason for the migration of rural people to the cities; there is always the hope, but never the certainty, of finding work.

Women bear the brunt

In many parts of the developing world men go to the city in search of work and women are left behind to carry the burden of farming and feeding their families. Moving to the city with their men may be a solution, but urban unemployment, without any "modern" skills, usually means continued poverty. Working as domestic servants or petty traders brings minimal financial rewards, and prostitution is an unpleasant option for a small minority.

Female-headed households are the most poverty-stricken group worldwide, and in Latin American cities they often represent up to 50 per cent of households. Even in a rich country such as the USA 78 per cent of people living below the official poverty line are women and children.

Boom and gloom: the poverty crisis

In the "boom" years of the 1980s, the number of people worldwide living in absolute poverty increased from 700 million in 1980 to about 1.2 billion by 1990. Thus, nearly a quarter of humanity lives in a state of virtual destitution. According to the Worldwatch Institute, more than 40 countries suffered reduced living standards in the 1980s, particularly in sub-Saharan Africa and South America. A major factor for this deterioration was and still is the huge burden of foreign debt. The net cash flow from the poor to the rich countries in the 1980s amounted to $50 billion annually, mainly due to debt repayments.

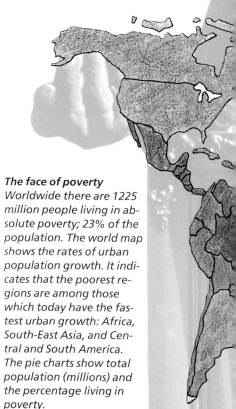

The face of poverty
Worldwide there are 1225 million people living in absolute poverty; 23% of the population. The world map shows the rates of urban population growth. It indicates that the poorest regions are among those which today have the fastest urban growth: Africa, South-East Asia, and Central and South America. The pie charts show total population (millions) and the percentage living in poverty.

"The urban poor are loosely tied in to a vicious circle of low capital, low training, shortage of remunerative work opportunities, and low incomes. Only a minority with considerable luck, talent, or initiative can break out of this situation, and the success of the minority is often conditional on the relative stagnation of the majority."

Joseph Gugler, *The Urbanization of the Third World*, 1988

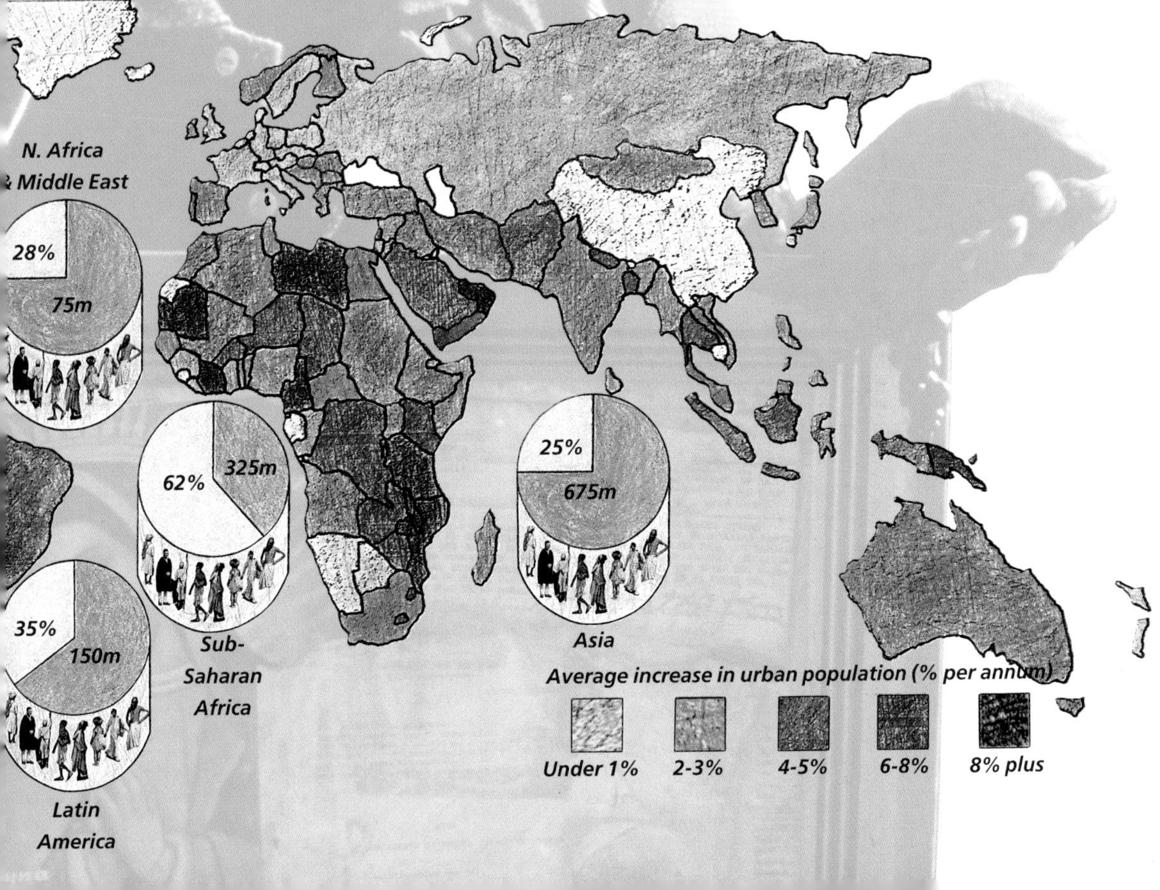

N. Africa & Middle East

28%

75m

Sub-Saharan Africa

62% 325m

Latin America

35% 150m

Asia

25%

675m

Average increase in urban population (% per annum)

Under 1%   2-3%   4-5%   6-8%   8% plus

Living on the street

Suffer the children

Children are worst affected by the horrors of absolute poverty: domestic insecurities, lack of play space, and poor nutrition are major contributing factors to their plight. Urban infant mortalities may be lower than in rural areas, but children's health is badly affected by inadequate, overcrowded surroundings.

In most developing-world cities, abandoned children are a fact of life. According to the Panos Institute in London there are about 100 million of them worldwide, with over 10,000 in Bangkok alone. In some cities, such as Nairobi, it is a crime to abandon children, but the realities of urban poverty have made the law ineffective, with no solution to the problem in sight.

With parents unable to afford proper schooling, many children drift into a life of street trading, begging and petty thieving, or work in sweat shops or as domestic servants at an early age. In Port-au-Prince, Haiti, about 200,000 children, known as restaveks ("live-withs"), work as domestics in slave-like conditions. Usually they have been sent to the city by parents unable to feed their many children on eroded plots of land.

Bangkok: child-selling and prostitution

In some countries conditions force parents to sell their children into virtual slavery. In Mauritania and Sudan it is possible to buy children for about $15. In Bangkok children are still sold as slaves to work in the sex industry or in sweatshops. Every year at the end of the harvest season, thousands of children, some as young as seven, arrive at the railway station. They are auctioned off for $150, or more if they are pretty girls, in which case they end up in brothels. Less attractive children are used as cheap labour.

The sex-tourist industry in Bangkok is a legacy of the Vietnam war, when American GIs took "relaxation" holidays there. Today at least 800,000 prostitutes between the ages of 10 and 16 work in Bangkok, while 80 per cent of all tourists to Thailand are single males, flying in on special package tours from Tokyo or Frankfurt.

The urban poor are invariably unskilled and under- or unemployed, or they pursue low-income service occupations such as barrow pushing, street trading, or shoe shining. The struggle to make "ends meet" is a cause of crime in many cities.

Entertaining the traffic
From washing windscreens in London to fire-eating in Mexico City: slow-moving cars are sitting targets worldwide.

Sâo Paulo:
murder after hours
The largest city in Brazil also has the largest population of street children, over 3 million in all, more than 10% of the city's population. Many of these children have been kicked out by their families, or have become displaced in the course of migration. The street kids make a precarious living as traders or thieves. They are at war with the police, some of whom prey on them in murder squads after duty hours.

Kathmandu:
police extortion
Nepal has a growing number of street children as a result of rural-urban migration. These children collect rubbish to make money, but are victimized by police, who extort money from them.

The rise and fall of the tower block

Right angles and straight lines

Forests of angular concrete monuments appeared on city skylines in the decades following World War II. A new coalition of architects, planners, and politicians had come to dominate the urban development scene. Vernacular building traditions, which had evolved slowly over centuries and were adapted to local materials and conditions, fell prey to the jaws of the bulldozer. New construction methods, using steel frames, reinforced concrete, and plate glass revolutionized architectural design.

Using "system building" techniques prefabricated concrete panels could be slotted together in a matter of weeks. However, the new towers were not just providing office space, but accommodation for families: supposedly a frontal assault on the problem of inadequate housing. Machines for living in, as Le Corbusier had called them (see pp. 56-7), were becoming a reality. From Berlin to Dresden, from Birmingham to Marseilles, from Detroit to Moscow and later in Sâo Paulo and other developing-world cities, the new towers mushroomed.

Community destruction

The clearance of traditional homes (see pp. 60-1) meant the destruction of the mutual support of community life. In the euphoria of creating a brave new world of housing projects, little effort was made to study the communities that were being obliterated. Rarely were people asked whether they wanted to move into a box in the sky. In Britain alone three million people were relocated from old urban neighbourhoods between 1955 and 1975.

Dwellers in the sky

As millions of people were moved into high-rise dwellings it became apparent that the tall, grey buildings often made unsuitable homes. The cold brutality of the architecture made the blocks feel bleak and comfortless, and alienation, loneliness, and stress became common experiences. Cramped apartments made life particularly difficult for families with young children. Lack of private space outside, and distance from the ground meant that children had nowhere to play supervised.

In 1972 the first high-rise housing project had to be demolished. The Pruitt-Igoe in St Louis, an award-winning housing project, which was completed in 1955, was dynamited because it was beyond redemption. Intended from the outset as housing for people removed from downtown ghettos, it was meant to have a better, greener ambience. But the 12,000 people who were decanted into the new estate felt otherwise. It was a cold, inhumane place consisting of 33 identical blocks. Space inside the apartments was minimal, and ventilation was inadequate. Old mattresses and furniture littered the streets and the stench of urine was ever-present. The dynamiting of Pruitt-Igoe set a trend since copied in other parts of the United States and Europe; hundreds of similar blocks have now been destroyed. However, other blocks were redesigned with the help of residents, providing facilities such as cafés, nurseries, and swimming pools. Self-management often led to greater acceptance of the blocks by residents, and a reduction in vandalism and crime.

"While 'slum clearance' was a powerful slogan in achieving the removal of old environments, it ignored the fact that most of the social problems found in slums were not directly related to their physical structure."

Prof. Hugh Freeman, University of Manchester

*"Glass, rubble and debris litter
the street, the accumulation is
astonishing . . . abandoned
automobiles have been left in
parking areas; glass is
omnipresent; tin cans are strewn
throughout, paper has been
rained on and stuck in the
cracked, hardened mud. Pruitt-
Igoe from without looks like a
disaster area."*

R. Montgomery, Pruitt-Igoe, 1985

Slum clearance: phase two
*Vandalized beyond repair, Tower
Hill flats (right) in Kirkby, Liverpool
were eventually demolished by
explosion in 1982.*

City stress

Sick buildings, sick people
Many blocks were badly built, poorly insulated, and damp. Leaky flat roofs, condensation on thin walls, rooms too hot in summer and too cold in winter were typical complaints and all contributed to general ill health, and chronic respiratory problems in particular. Stress-related illnesses were also commonplace. And in such out-sized, inhospitable buildings the fear of violence was never far away. The dimly lit walkways, passages, and corridors seemed tailor-made for lurking muggers and the breakdown of lifts or failure of electricity supplies caused people to be stranded, adding to their feelings of helplessness.

Built-in stress
Living high up was found to be more stressful than living on the ground. Many people developed a fear of heights and open spaces, often taking refuge in tranquillizers, alcohol, and other drugs. In studies conducted in Britain the incidence of psychoneurotic disorders was found to be three times higher among residents of multi-storeyed dwellings than among those living in low-level detached houses, and the higher up people lived the greater the likelihood of stress.

Living in crowded conditions (see pp. 72-3) can also be experienced as a potent form of stress. Some researchers have suggested that individuals with less than eight square metres of living space suffer from increased anxiety levels. But living in crowded high-rise conditions is not universally experienced as causing intolerable stress. In Hong Kong and Singapore where high-rise living is the norm, people appear to cope far more successfully. Better design of blocks, better supervision, and mutual support of large, extended families are factors in the greater success of high-rise buildings in these cities.

Dumping grounds
In many parts of the world high-rise developments became dumping grounds for the less fortunate in society. Drug use, crime, and vandalism contributed to deteriorating social conditions on "problem" developments.

Cities are stressful places. Stress can be caused by a number of factors, but people's inability to control their close environment is perhaps the most significant. The sheer number of people in crowds, high noise levels, and fumes are all causes of tension and stress. Urban environments also cause an "information overload" with myriad flashing lights, signals, advertising, shop window displays, and fast-moving vehicles making constant demands on peoples' attention. All this, together with "existential anxieties" and employment worries, inadequate housing, and unstable human relationships cause many urban people to live at the limits of exhaustion. Some people become aggressive and prone to violence, and drug addiction and alcoholism are predictable responses to feelings of extreme insecurity.

"High blocks are regarded as creating anonymity because they segregate people at different levels instead of allowing the normal interactions that take place on the street when houses are on the ground. The anonymity produces feelings of loneliness and isolation, and . . . may produce neuroses."

Alice Coleman, *Utopia on Trial*, 1990

"Debbie is an optimistic person... she says how lucky she has been...to have survived a suicide attempt with 50 para-cetamols.... What she cannot talk about easily is the pain behind her drinking problem..."

The Independent,
5 February 1992

Unpopular they may be, but tower blocks still exist and people still have to live in them. The problems remain unchanged.

Chain reaction of urban decline

By the late 1960s the great urban manufacturing centres of the USA and Britain had started to "deindustrialize", losing out to competition from countries such as Japan and Germany. North American cities shed 38 million manufacturing jobs between 1969 and 1976. Cities in Britain were similarly affected, and London lost over 800,000 jobs between 1971 and 1982. Smaller companies could only partially compensate for the decline of the urban-industrial base. As unemployment spread so did money worries, marital tensions, depression, and stress. Drug addiction, alcoholism, and violence were all responses to extreme stress, as were serious health problems such as chronic heart disease. The combination of inhumane environments, poor housing conditions, insecurity, family breakdown, and high unemployment led to the contemporary social pathology expressed in record crime rates.

Vandalism: expression of no hope

Unemployed young people suffered most of all. With nothing to do and few prospects, boredom, disorientation, and financial worries began to shape their behaviour. In the 1970s the industrial recession in the USA saw vandalism rise by 70 per cent. Today its incidence is greatest in inner-city areas of high unemployment, high population turnover, poor-quality housing, and concentrations of underprivileged ethnic minorities. Graffiti is one of the less aggressive forms of "routine" vandalism, but ripping up park benches and subway seats, or smashing telephone booths is commonplace.

Youth gangs: a response to city stress

In many North American cities young people find it nearly impossible to get work and youth gangs, a common phenomenon, are the results of marginalization and of the "juvenization of poverty". In Los Angeles unemployment among young blacks during the late 1980s averaged 45%. Over 300 gangs have been identified by the Los Angeles police department and black, Irish, Latino, Chinese, Cambodian, and Filipino gangs all have their own separate identities and clearly defined territories. With the continuing erosion of jobs due to the closure of steel mills, aerospace industries, and many other sources of employment, gangs emerged in many parts of the city. In the 1980s youth gangs became involved in a major international trade – crack. Crack dealing is closely associated with LA street gangs such as the Crips and the Bloods dating back to the 1970s. In Los Angeles an estimated 10,000 people are involved in crack trading. Its very addictiveness has created a sustained market, providing as much employment as several automobile factories. But street earnings from crack are usually well below $1000 a month. Only "drug czars" can afford a gleaming BMW or Mercedes.

"Gangs are never goin' to die out. You all goin' to get us jobs?"

Black youth in Los Angeles

"Riots are the language of the unheard."

Martin Luther King

". . . everywhere in the inner city, even in the forgotten poor-white boondocks with their zombie populations of speed-freaks, gangs are multiplying at a terrifying rate, cops are becoming more arrogant and trigger-happy, and a whole generation is being shunted towards some impossible Armageddon."

Mike Davis, *City of Quartz*, 1990

Mexican gang: Los Angeles
Street gangs "control" substantial areas of the city (below), "reclaiming" what was once Mexican territory.

CHAPTER 4

The city as parasite

City dependency

A parasite is an organism that lives, and is dependent on, another host, from which it is nourished. Cities fit this description perfectly. They are dependent on a steady flow of supplies from the world's farmlands, forests, and fishing grounds, without which they simply could not exist. Ever more artificial ecosystems are created for producing maximum food and timber yields, employing industrial production methods. Unfortunately these are often obtained using environmentally damaging and highly polluting techniques of production and disposal. The actual environmental costs of urban consumption patterns are still unacknowledged in the purchase price of commercial products and processed foods (see pp. 92-3).

The energy drain

Everywhere fossil fuels are vital links in an increasingly unstable chain of production and supply. Cities are at the centre of this. The energy that flows through them today is at least a hundred times greater than that which flows through natural, unmanipulated ecosystems. Using fossil fuel deposits as their main source of fuel, cities rely on internal combustion engines and power stations to supply nearly all their energy needs (see pp. 106-7). Not only are these dependent on non-renewable resources but their combustion produces waste gases that are affecting the wellbeing of the biosphere and the Earth's atmosphere. Acid-rain damaged forests and global warming are, above all else, caused by the fuel consumption patterns of modern cities.

City of waste

The vast outputs generated by cities in the form of gaseous, liquid, and solid wastes are the result of a lack of understanding of the need to make cities sustainable. Industrial pollution, in particular, can leave environmental legacies that people will have to deal with for generations to come. Cities are bad *parasites* because at present they have little concern for the health of their host organism, Gaia, the living planet Earth. If their functioning damages Gaia, they too will be severely affected.

The global supermarket

Rich cities have the world as their supermarket. Supplies come from the cheapest source, regardless of the environmental consequences of exploiting resources. The price of urbanization today is virtually unrestricted access to forests, farmland, and water supplies. Fossil fuels from the Earth's crust, deposited over millions of years, are being exploited for use by mainly urban consumers in a matter of a few decades. But supermarkets usually fail to inform the consumer about the true origin of things that go into the shopping trolley and consumers are not encouraged to ask.

City of gluttony
The greedy city pushes its over-loaded trolley down the global supermarket aisle, gathering extravagant supplies, and leaving in its wake devastated ecosystems.

Urban demands

Cities are the main consumers of forest products – charcoal, timber, and pulp. In the past cities had their own local forests to supply their needs, but most cities today don't have such a convenient arrangement. As cities grow, they prey initially on forests on their own doorsteps, but then they have to look further and further afield to satisfy their needs. Forest cover on Earth has shrunk from 90 per cent in ancient times to less than 25 per cent today, mainly because of urban demand for forest products and farmland. Different types of cities have different requirements and consumption patterns: many cities of the developing world still rely on fuelwood, but consume very little paper, while more developed cities use large amounts of paper and little fuelwood. All cities require supplies of timber for building materials and furniture.

The effects of deforestation

Deforestation has very serious environmental consequences. Tree roots bind soil together, and on sloping land in particular, loss of tree cover leads to soil erosion, which causes loss of top soil and may also cause contamination and silting of surface waters with soil. Large-scale deforestation in hot countries can result in a substantial increase in soil temperature, making it unsuitable for certain crops. In tropical forests, daytime temperatures are typically around 26°C, but with forest cover removed, temperatures can rise by up to 10°C. Deforestation over large areas can also cause a significant loss of ambient moisture.

Tropical forests have been called the world's air conditioners but in the last few decades they have shrunk by some 50 per cent, recently at the annual rate of 17 million hectares, which is an area of land almost the size of Britain. Climate change, due in part to forest destruction, resulting from reduced moisture levels, higher temperatures, and increased carbon dioxide (CO_2) levels in the atmosphere is a global issue (see also pp. 112-13), affecting the quality of life worldwide.

Chainsaw massacre

Today rich cities take it for granted that they can get low-cost timber supplies from forests somewhere, anywhere, on Earth. Softwood requirements are met mainly from countries such as Canada, Sweden,

Paragominas – sawmill capital of the world

Located on the Brasilia-Belém highway Paragominas, with a population of 40,000 people, has some 500 mills using several thousand trees from the virgin forest every day. The cut trees are worth perhaps $100 each, but by the time they are sold as planks in London or Frankfurt they can be worth tens of thousands. In addition, harvest offcuts, often perfectly good mahogany planks, or even trees straight from virgin forest are taken to make charcoal. This is used for smelting pig iron using iron ore from the nearby Carajas mine. Much of this pig iron is exported to Germany and Japan, to be used for making cars.

"Forests on the whole are simply being mined away, taking out the easiest to get – and the most highly priced trees – without any real concern for what happens afterwards."

A. Leslie, *Unasylva Magazine*, 29, 1977

Finland, and increasingly, Siberia. Hardwood imports used to come from tropical forests in Ghana, Ivory Coast, the Philippines, and Thailand, but today these places have few trees left. So instead, Malaysia, Indonesia, Papua New Guinea, and Brazil have become leading suppliers of tropical hardwoods to cities such as Tokyo, Singapore, and the cities of western Europe.

Deforestation is often considered to be a rural problem. But, urban people in the developed countries unwittingly deplete and destroy vast areas of forest every year as they "harmlessly" acquire hardwood front doors, double glazing frames, or plywood panelling.

Record timber consumer

Japan holds the world record in tropical timber imports. In 1987 she imported over 20 million cubic metres of timber, 53 per cent of all tropical hardwood traded on the world market. Most of the wood came from countries in the region such as Malaysia and Indonesia, but also from the Amazon. Much of the timber is used in house construction, since traditional Japanese homes are built of wood. The average life span of buildings in Tokyo today is little over five years! The attitude now is that buildings are disposable items, easily replaced by taller ones, whenever necessary. Vast quantities of tropical plywood are wasted in shuttering as concrete is poured and left to set. After being used two or three times, the plywood is thrown away.

Rings of deforestation

Many large cities, such as Nairobi, Khartoum, Delhi, Ouagadougou, Dakar, and Niamey, have, in their quest for wood, deforested large rings around themselves. Many cities in the developing world still rely heavily on firewood and charcoal for fuel and villages in the vicinity of big cities are often profoundly affected by this urban demand. African cities, in particular, are surrounded by areas from which nearly all mature trees have been removed – extending to 100km or more – leaving local villagers and farmers without adequate firewood. In Tanzania most industries are concentrated in Dar-es-Salaam, the former capital city. Since it relies on regular supplies of firewood as its chief energy source, it competes with nearby villages for this vital resource.

India's fuelwood crisis

India's cities use vast quantities of firewood – over 16 million tonnes were consumed in Indian cities in 1984 – even though kerosene is commonly available and cooking with firewood is actually more expensive. Kerosene stoves are valuable items and many people's homes are not secure enough to prevent them from being stolen. Delhi, like other cities, has largely exhausted local supplies of firewood, and today has to import it from distant forests in Madhya Pradesh, Assam, and Bihar. Each year about 224,000 tonnes of firewood are unloaded at railway sidings to be taken to the city.

Who uses the paper?

Per capita annual paper consumption per country

Country	kg
USA	268
UK	124
France	115
Thailand	11
Egypt	10
India	2

Thirsty cities

Cities, particularly those of developed countries, require vast quantities of water. Worldwide, North American citizens use the most, with an average daily use of nearly 6400 litres, a figure that includes water used domestically, for land irrigation, and for industry. Traditionally most early cities drew on water from nearby rivers and lakes, but modern cities are often built in less suitable locations, with limited local water augmented by supplies from remote sources. "Fossil" water from underground aquifers is one source, but dams and pipelines are more important.

Pipelines in the desert

California, a mainly urban state, with 30 million inhabitants and a $700-billion economy, exists courtesy of water pipelines. Cities such as Los Angeles, San Diego, and San Jose have scant rainfall and could not survive without water pipes. Los Angeles, for example, taps the Owens River 400km away. The state has 1300 major dams, many of which supply water as well as electricity. But some water comes from even further afield, through a pipeline from the Colorado river basin. The California Aqueduct is so huge it is the only man-made object visible from the moon.

Beyond natural limits

Eighty-five per cent of water piped to California is used for its $18 billion agricultural business, producing mainly water-guzzling crops such as citrus fruits, rice, and cotton. Cattle yards and the beef produced from irrigated fields depend entirely on piped water. The pipelines and the under-ground aquifers have made the desert bloom, but at a price. As in ancient Sumeria (see pp. 40-1), the poorly drained irrigated fields of California are now becoming salty. The few drainage channels in use wash salt, toxic selenium, and fertilizer residues into lower-lying regions, causing a build-up of toxins there instead. Meanwhile California's inhabitants are demanding even more water to maintain their sub-tropical dream gardens, where sprinklers do the job of rainclouds.

Turning on the tap

Large dams have to be constructed to supply water and power to cities. Dams have been built since 1945 and the tallest, at 300 metres, is on the River Vakh in the USSR. With dams costing many millions of dollars, developing-world countries have to take on massive loans that they can ill afford, particularly if the dam then fails. Even if it succeeds, the water supply may actually be below the level of the city it is supplying. For example, Mexico City relies for much of its water on dams 1000 metres below it and the water has to be pumped up to the city at enormous energy costs.

Upstream
Above the dam, fertile river valleys are flooded, displacing farmers, who are often forced to farm on sloping ground, stripping trees to grow crops, with soil erosion an inevitable consequence. The stagnant water means exposure to diseases such as malaria and leishmaniasis.

The Balbina dam, Brazil
This was built to supply Manaus with electricity. Damming the River Uatuma flooded 2500 sq km of rainforest. Few trees were felled before the dam was erected and the acid water from decaying trees suffocated fish and corroded the turbines. The area also became a breeding ground for malarial mosquitoes. The local Waimiri tribe was decimated; its land was flooded and the people exposed to new diseases. At a cost of $700 million, borrowed from foreign banks, Balbina is an economic disaster. It will never be able to pay its way, yet the money borrowed will have to be repaid. The dam produces far less electricity than planned and Manaus already needs another dam.

Downstream
Dams are usually built to expand areas of irrigated farmland. In the developing world small communities near hydroelectric dams are often without electricity, with supplies being reserved for use by cities.

The hidden cost of cheap food

Cities demand cheap food

Since the days of ancient Rome, cities have demanded cheap food (see also pp. 42-3) and today, as the world's major food consumers, cities are able to drive a hard bargain. Food for cities comes from wherever it is cheapest, even if this is half way around the world.

Meat production for urban use often means that animals are kept in intensive units. Their sole function is to grow, be killed, and eaten as quickly as possible. Large monocultures of animals are inherently unstable, and the constant use of, chemicals, antibiotics, and other medicines is necessary to keep diseases and pests at bay, but residues from the chemicals used can contaminate food and are a worry for many people.

Urban food appeal

People not only demand cheap food, they want it to look good too, and expect unblemished food in standardized presentation. Advertisements reveal the visual attraction, not the nutritional value, of food, and growers are under pressure to produce a few "popular" varieties, sold for their looks and ability to withstand mechanized harvesting, and lengthy transport and storage periods.

The standardization of food in monoculture crops invariably means the liberal use of pesticides to prevent crop disease. Pesticide residues in food are a danger to the consumer but farmers applying pesticides are at greater risk. In 1983, the World Health Organisation estimated an annual global figure of two million pesticide poisonings, including some 4000 fatalities.

The global food industry

The rural hinterland of many cities today extends right around the globe. Since Roman days bread has been an urban staple food and this is true even for cities in areas where wheat cannot be grown. For example, the bread sold in Lagos is likely to have been made from Kansas wheat. The global trade in food and animal feed has become routine, since transport costs are relatively low, but can the Earth afford to supply us with food at bargain prices?

Urban dwellers in the developed world spend no more than 15 to 20% of their income on food. But the price we pay does not represent the true cost of the food we eat. Soil erosion, land deterioration, water contamination, and damage to rural ecosystems by modern farming methods are not included in the price. Large cities and large mechanized farms go hand in hand as modern urban industries supply farmers with the technological ingredients for producing food cheaply. Cheap food means maximum use of machinery and minimal labour costs. Farm workers displaced from the land by new technologies swell the urban millions worldwide.

Before
Prior to extensive urban growth, mixed, labour-intensive family farms were the rule. Fields were enclosed by hedges; woodlands and pastures dotted the land. People grew crops for their own use, and sold surpluses in local markets.

After
Modern farming systems produce standardized crops. They have inferior nutrient value, and the soil quality deteriorates.

The urban food machine
City gents now control the farms not the farmers. Hi-tech aids – tractors, combine harvesters, artificial fertilizers, and pesticides – help destroy a thousand-year-old peasant way of life.

Separation from the land

Throughout the world farmland has been traditionally replenished by animal and human body wastes (see also pp. 162-5) – a great asset because they contain all the plant nutrients required to grow the crops we eat. The growth of cities has usually caused the separation of people from the land on which their food is grown. This makes it difficult to return the nutrients consumed by city dwellers back to the land. Once nutrients and minerals have been removed from farmland, as crops are harvested, and not returned to refertilize the soil, the land becomes proportionately less productive.

The trouble with disposal

The fact that sewage is a valuable substance seems to have been largely forgotten by sewage engineers. Disposal rather than recycling has been their brief since the 19th century when waterborne systems were widely introduced. In those days the prime concern was to move sewage out of harm's way, so that people would not come into contact with it and diseases such as cholera could be prevented. But effective sewage treatment is expensive and even today many cities cannot or will not pay up.

Sewage treatment

Sewage systems today are designed to process a mixture of human and industrial wastes to make them "harmless"; waste goes through a series of treatments. However they are insufficient for industrial societies, with their mixed household and factory effluents. Sewage sludge is disposed of by ocean-dumping, land-filling, spreading on agricultural land, incinerating, or by composting. But it is often contaminated and therefore dangerous to living beings. Undesirable toxic chemicals are used during waste treatment; chlorine is used in ammonia control, but the treatment often fails to remove heavy metals and synthetic chemicals discharged by industry. Today 20-70,000 manufactured chemical substances are released into the environment, many ending up contaminating water courses such as rivers, lakes, estuaries, and coastal waters (see also pp. 100-1).

Down the fertility drain

The food consumption of cities has become a drain on the fertility of farmland. In the mid-19th century the German chemist Liebig tried to persuade Europe's growing cities not to build sewage-disposal systems, but recycling systems instead. He did not succeed; he then set out to develop artificial fertilizers. Today it is clearer than ever that we cannot afford to keep flushing away valuable plant nutrients.

Principle of recycling
In nature everything is recycled; for cities to become sustainable they have to follow the same principle.

Essential nutrients
The main nutrients removed from the soil by growing crops are nitrogen, potash, phosphates, magnesium, and calcium. They end up in urban sewage and should be recycled, not dumped.

Hazards of untreated sewage
Cities use water to flush away liquid wastes, but they are often untreated, putting people at risk from cholera, typhoid, intestinal parasites, and dysentery. Disposal of sewage in water-courses also causes an oversupply of nutrients, causing eutrophication, followed by a loss of oxygen, which kills aquatic life.

Sewage in the developing world
Many developing-world cities are overwhelmed by the amount of sewage they generate. Squatter camps are often inadequately serviced and people are forced to relieve themselves on the streets. The very fertility of human wastes makes them a rich breeding ground for diseases. In Lima in 1991 a major outbreak of cholera occurred, which has since spread to many other areas in Latin America. Mexico City is one of them. Many of the shanties there have no sewage system, and hundreds of tonnes of dry faeces, suspended in the air, pose a constant health threat.

The chemical threat

The legacy of industry

The very prosperity of modern, industrial cities depends on production processes involving substances dangerous to life. The ever-growing demand for industrially produced goods is being met at substantial costs to the environment and human health. Coke works, lead smelters, and tanneries, paper and textile mills, fertilizer factories, and petrochemical complexes all release highly toxic substances.

The location scandal

While increasingly stringent environmental laws have curbed emissions in developed countries, cities in the developing world, where legislation is lax, often suffer from appalling pollution. To make matters worse many large companies relocate their more dangerous production processes to developing-world cities.

The Indian city of Bhopal has become an international symbol for pollution and death. Hundreds of thousands of people were settled in shacks around the Union Carbide pesticide factory there. When bad maintenance and carelessness led to the explosion of the factory in 1984, some 3000 people were killed and about 40,000 were maimed, with chronic lung and eye damage.

The poor suffer

Factories are usually located in or close to cities and it is the poorest areas, particularly in developing-world cities that are the worst affected by pollution, since communities grow up around the factories as people flock to them for work. These settlements are in constant danger from air pollution, since they are invariably located downwind of the chimneys; whereas the rich can buy their way into upwind areas. Polluted air flows freely into squatter homes and vegetation that helps to filter air is usually absent. Water may have to be collected from sources close to factory outfall pipes and soil may be contaminated with lead, mercury, and chlorinated compounds. Diarrhoea, skin diseases, tuberculosis, bronchial problems, emphysema, and many other diseases are commonplace.

The modern chemical industry presents particularly bad pollution problems. Many of its products are made of chlorinated hydrocarbons, the manufacture of which involves the breakdown of salt into soda and chlorine. Combined with oil-derived liquids, these materials are then synthesized into plastics, pesticides, fertilizers, and pharmaceuticals. The manufacture, use, and disposal of chlorinated hydrocarbons invariably causes contamination problems. In addition, poisonous heavy metals such as mercury and cadmium, used in the production of chemicals, are released into the environment.

Cubatao: city of pollution
In Brazil the industrial city of Cubatao, near Sâo Paulo and the port of Santos, is a major centre for chemicals' manufacture and heavy industry, many of which are subsidiaries of multinationals. Until recently the city was notorious for extremely high industrial pollution levels – large numbers of people suffered chronic pneumonia, tuberculosis, bronchitis, and emphysema. Air, soil, and water pollution also led to very high rates of stillborn and deformed babies and childhood cancer was at a record high. Children had to go to hospital to breathe in medicated air. Play areas were found to be contaminated with highly dangerous chemicals. Recently a clean-up has improved the situation slightly.

"The colonial countries are nothing but a dumping ground and pool of cheap labor for capitalist corporations. . . . The costs are simply borne by . . . the victims of Union Carbide, Dow, and Standard Oil."

" 'We thought it was a plague', said one victim. Indeed it was: a chemical plague, an industrial plague."

George Bradford, "We all live in Bhopal"

Living in the shadow of industry
Children in Mexico City (above) play on a railway line running past an industrial site.

Mountains of rubbish

Co-disposal – making matters worse

Cities today are prodigious producers of waste. Disposing of vast quantities of waste is a major problem complicated by mixing different materials together. The waste collection process in most cities still does not separate out materials. Kitchen wastes, plastics, paper, aluminium, batteries, and oils are all thrown into the same dump, each type of waste releasing its own breakdown products as it rots. To make things worse, many cities co-dispose household and factory waste, the theory being that household waste soaks up any toxins in the factory waste. This toxic cocktail is a costly legacy for generations to come. In addition, pollution of groundwater is a problem wherever rubbish is dumped, and dumps give off methane, an explosive and highly potent greenhouse gas. Even if waste tips are sealed at great expense, the complex mixture they contain will take decades to decompose.

Aluminium cans – what a waste

The post-war era saw the extensive use of aluminium for packaging. In 1963, when aluminium was first used for disposable beverage cans, one billion were produced in the USA – about five per person. By 1985 up to 66 billion cans were used annually.

Aluminium production requires huge amounts of energy. Added to this, most aluminium comes from bauxite deposits in the tropics; huge areas of rainforest have been destroyed not only to make room for open bauxite mining but also for hydroelectric dams (see pp. 90-1) and reservoirs to power the mining operations.

Wasted food

Waste food should ideally be returned to farms and fed to livestock, or composted and used to fertilize garden soil, but very few city dwellers are able to do this. Most of the food eaten in cities is packaged in plastics and cardboard, further contributing to the waste problem.

Managing waste is a skill that we have yet to acquire. But what we should really be learning is how to stop creating so much waste in the first place.

The richer the city, the more waste each citizen throws away. New York holds the world waste record, with 1.60kg per person per day. Every day the city has to dispose of 24,000 tonnes of trash. Europeans throw away about half the amount that Americans do, while in developing-world cities, although the amount thrown away is high, the recycling rate is also high, with many people eking out a living as scavengers. In some cities, such as Jakarta, scavenging is encouraged to help solve the rubbish disposal problem.

Municipal waste
The chart shows that rich cities, as expected, generate far more waste than poor ones.

Population (millions)

Kilogrammes of rubbish per day (millions)

23
22
21
20
19
18
17
16
15
14
13
12
11
10
9
8
7
6
5
4
3
2
1
0

| Rome | Lahore | Hong Kong | Karachi | London | Calcutta | Los Angeles | New York | Mexico City | Tokyo Yokohama |

The deadly liquid

Water contamination

As centres of industry and of consumption cities often cause appalling water contamination problems. Rivers, especially, have become the victims of urban-industrial-agricultural discharges, containing the full range of toxins we release from factories, households, and farms. Examinations of coastal regions exposed to urban effluents usually reveal greatly depleted eco-systems.

The River Po: a convenient sewer

As the River Po reaches the plains of northern Italy it picks up effluents containing paint solvents, bleaches, oil, and household sewage from large industrial cities such as Turin. To the east the river flows through some of Europe's most productive farmland, where the ingredients of our favourite Italian dishes are grown using hi-tech farming methods with heavy dosages of fertilizers and pesticides. Slurry from factory-farmed beef cattle seeps into the groundwater and eventually into the river. As it reaches the Adriatic this mixture of urban, factory, and farming effluents, rich in both nutrients and poisons, is highly toxic. Beaches are often littered with dead fish and the water covered with smelly algal blooms.

The Baltic: an enclosed receptacle

Large lakes and inland oceans are receptacles for fertilizer run-off and carelessly discarded industrial and urban effluents. Of the many rivers that discharge into the Baltic the Vistula is the greatest polluter. As the river reaches the sea it is virtually dead, bringing with it the residues of Poland's appallingly dirty industries. Waste water treatment is virtually unheard of and salt from Poland's lignite mines makes stretches of the river saltier than the Baltic. This water is too corrosive even to be used for industrial cooling. Copper mines, aluminium smelters, refineries, and the defense industries are all located along the river, a convenient waste water conduit. Warsaw itself has no sewage treatment of any kind, so raw sewage ends up in the Baltic, together with the usual load of nitrates, phosphates, pesticides, and slurry.

Industrial, agricultural, and household effluents containing heavy metals, bleaches, oil residues, fertilizers, and pesticides pass through the same sewage systems as human wastes. Like a poisoned bait this potent brew can both stimulate and kill aquatic life. Nitrates and phosphates over-enrich water, causing eutrophication. Persistent pollutants accumulate as they pass up the food chain, and it is those animals at the top of the chain, including humans, that are worst affected from regular consumption of contaminated seafood.

Leaking city waste dumps
Urban waste dumps leach out deadly chemical cocktails, which seep into the groundwater and rivers. In New Jersey many wells are contaminated with leacheate from buried factory wastes and consumers suffer increased levels of chronic ailments and cancer.

The toxic cocktail
The ingredients of the cocktail we serve up to algae, fish, and other aquatic organisms are common to rivers and coastal waters worldwide. Phenol, cyanide, arsenic, heavy metals, sulphates, and chlorine compounds all build up in body tissues, causing disease and death.

The risk to fish
Fish often have no choice but to swallow toxic chemicals. Fish may no longer be jumping for joy, but due to a lack of oxygen or excess ammonia or chlorine. Sturgeon now avoid Russia's polluted River Volga.

The car in the mind

Cars rule the world

An alien from space visiting a modern city could be forgiven for believing that cars are its "real" inhabitants. Seen from the air at night cars dominate the urban landscape, their roving headlamps creating ribbons of light. During the day, cars are more apparent than people, "resting" bumper to bumper on city streets. The alien might conclude that the city was largely designed for the benefit of cars, having the use of roads and motorways much wider than the pavements on which people are confined.

Visions of freedom

Since car ownership has become universal in developed countries, we have gradually organized our lives around the distances we can travel. Our very existence is now so bound up with the motor car that we can hardly envisage life without it. The freedom to go where we like when we like is now accepted as a given right. Our city mind-maps are becoming progressively larger as the car shrinks distances and time. Children become accustomed to cars from birth and in the West are more likely to be able to identify different brands of car than different trees or flowers.

The major polluters

Today's motor vehicles cause massive air pollution (see pp. 108-11). This affects human health and also causes significant damage to trees and crops. In addition to nitrogen oxides (NOx), hydrocarbons, and carbon monoxide (CO), cars also release huge amounts of carbon dioxide (CO_2). A single tank of petrol produces between 120 and 180 kg of CO_2. Motor vehicle traffic today is responsible for about 15 per cent of the world's CO_2 output. Concentrations of NOx in the air have been rising and the trend seems set to continue.

Air pollution from vehicles has been worsening worldwide. In the 1980s the economic boom led to a substantial increase in car ownership and vehicle use in the developed world. In 1992, 600 million motor vehicles were in use worldwide. Bumper-to-bumper traffic jams belching out exhaust fumes are a feature of cities the world over.

Cars are addictive. As we learn to rely on them, they refuse to let go of us. As our hands grip the steering wheel, control, power, and "freedom" are within our grasp. Inside our cosy home on wheels, the thrill of speed turns even the mild-mannered into self-styled rally drivers. Fast cars are the manifestation of the "amplified man", whose feet have become wheels, whose muscles have been replaced by motors. Cars induce an unreal state of mind. As the world whizzes by we are lulled away from mundane worries. But traffic jams and accidents kill such illusions: the darker side of car use that we try to forget. "Grid locks" can literally turn people crazy, screaming with frustration, with their destination just out of reach.

"He who sows streets and multi-storey car parks harvests traffic jams."

Daniel Goeudevert,
Volkswagen
Manager, Germany

Long-distance haulage

In Europe the liberalization of trade is leading to a steady increase in long-distance lorry transport between urban centres. Lorry diesel engines emit NOx as well as fine soot particles, which are implicated in lung cancer. While there is now a legal obligation to fit all new petrol cars with catalytic converters by 1993, emissions from diesel-powered vehicles are not being curbed significantly. The European Commission's Task Force on the Environment has stated that it considers transport as the most important single source of environmental damage. But only about one-eighth of the social and environmental costs of lorry transport are actually paid for by the haulier. Noise pollution, vibration, accidents, demand for road and parking space, and above all exhaust emissions are paid for by society and by the natural environment.

Cities in the age of the car

Cities built since the invention of the car are shaped by its presence and their inhabitants' reliance on it. Los Angeles, Brasilia, and Milton Keynes are just three such cities. Their low-density layout reflects the planners' assumptions that people would all own their own cars, live highly mobile lifestyles, and drive great distances daily. This attitude takes no account of the elderly, the young, the poor, and non-drivers. Such cities were planned with a freeway system to facilitate car movement, but they also take up more space.

LA: without a car, you're nowhere

Los Angeles, with 11 million people, covers an area almost three times the size of metropolitan London, with roughly the same population. The city started growing along its network of electric railways, but a vast road system of 21,000km of arterial highways, 2000 of which are freeways, has been built since World War II. Two-thirds of journeys are made by private transport. Those few who use public transport endure inefficiency and inconvenience. Cars running on cheap petrol have shaped the city, making possible a sprawling layout based on large private plots and detached houses.

Car facts

- In the US the car industry uses one-fifth of the country's steel and two-thirds of its rubber.
- In 1988 the world's 400 million cars pumped 500 million tonnes of carbon into the atmosphere.
- 15% of carbon from fossil fuels is burned by cars.
- In the US nearly 11.5 billion litres of gasoline were burned up in traffic jams in 1984, 4% of annual consumption.
- In the US every kilometre of freeway takes up a total of 6 hectares of land.

● Nearly one-third of land in cities is devoted to cars.
● In London rush hour traffic averages only 19km per hour – about the same as in Bombay.
● In 1985 more than 250,000 people died in traffic accidents worldwide.

"Worldwide, more than one new car is produced every second. Spend the night in bed and when you wake up the next morning 30,000 new cars will have been made while you were asleep. In 1989 world car production topped 35 million vehicles a year."

Greenpeace UK, "Mad Car Disease"

Spaghetti junction, Los Angeles
The archetypal car city, with its space-eating freeway junctions (below), also pioneered transport pollution problems.

Points of light

Modern cities are products of cheap energy. Nothing illustrates the fossil fuel dependence of cities better than seeing cities at night. Millions upon millions of light bulbs – advertising signs, street lights, and domestic lights – are energized by power stations. The streaks of light from the headlamps of the myriad cars complete the picture.

Cities run on coal, oil, and gas

The rapid growth of cities in the 19th century followed equally rapid advances in coal mining. Between 1850 and 1913 the per capita annual consumption of coal in British cities went up from 1.7 to 4 tonnes. In recent years energy consumption has gone up even faster: commercial energy use in US cities went up by an average of 5.6 per cent per year between 1960 and 1980, closely following rates of economic growth.

Coal is important for the generation of electricity, and oil has become the lifeblood of contemporary cities – powering their road transport. Natural gas, mainly used since 1945, is now a major source of energy supplies in modern cities.

The wasted resource

Contemporary megacities would not exist without fossil fuels. As primary consumers cities use up fossil fuels hundreds of thousands of times faster than they can accumulate in the Earth. Cities are also responsible for a colossal wastage of energy. Electricity is supplied from power stations that can be less than 30 per cent efficient; over 70 per cent of their fuel energy is wasted in the generation and transmission of electricity.

Energy for developing-world cities

The booming growth of developing-world cities has also relied on the availability of fossil fuels. The era of cheap oil led to a boom in demand even in poorer countries. But the spiralling price of oil in the 1970s brought back a dependence on wood fuel. Today these cities burn substantial amounts of firewood and charcoal again, dangerously depleting dwindling local forests (see pp. 88-9).

The energy costs of urban sprawl

The distances involved in bringing in the supplies needed by cities would be inconceivable without the transport infrastructure based on cheap oil. Without oil cities, particularly large, low-density ones would grind to a halt. Cars and public transport have shaped our sprawling conurbations, with commuter suburbs now an integral feature of cities. Energy savings would be possible

in cities if the car was renounced in
favour of public transport. Fuel can
only be burned once; if it is burned
today it will not be available tomorrow. Their very dependence on non-
renewable resources makes cities
vulnerable to future
supplies' shortages.

The lights of Las Vegas
*Millions of energy-guzzling
light bulbs adorn the clubs
and casinos of Las Vegas
(below), obviating the
need for street lights.*

Urban fumes and human health

One-fifth of humankind, over one billion people, live in places, particularly megacities, where the air is not fit to breathe. Atmospheric pollution in cities comes from a number of sources. Households burning coal, still the case in eastern Europe and much of Asia, cause cities to be cloaked in great plumes of sulphurous smoke. Before the Clean Air Act in 1955, London suffered from dense winter smogs – in 1952 some 4000 people died from their effects. Today a less visible cocktail of thousands of poisonous gases is given off by modern factories, refineries, power stations, and aeroplanes. Together with exhaust fumes given off by motor vehicles they are a new cause for respiratory diseases and chronic conditions such as asthma.

Urban air pollution in Chinese cities

In countries with large coal deposits urban air pollution is a major problem. The plumes of smoke over Chinese cities are so dense that sometimes the cities are not visible on satellite photographs: the people call the smog the "yellow dragon". China burns 900 million tonnes of coal every year, about 80 per cent of its total energy consumption. The price of coal is very low, so there is no incentive to burn it efficiently. Since the coal has a very high sulphur content of some five per cent, urban air pollution in China is highly acidic. Scrubbers for cleaning sulphur from flue gases are, as yet, non-existent in China.

The bad breath of our cities

Air pollution from cities is in urgent need of being cleaned up because it now envelops whole continents. Urban and industrial haze from European and American cities is being detected as far north as the Arctic Circle. In recent years astronauts have observed an ever-thickening veil of yellow haze over the face of the Earth, thickest close to major industrial centres.

Damage to our forests

In the early 1980s substantial damage to trees was first noticed in Germany. Today right across Europe

The fuming city

Metropolitan Mexico is regarded as the city with the worst air pollution on Earth. It is four times worse than Los Angeles, and six times higher than is acceptable under World Health Authority standards. Part of the reason is that polluted air cannot disperse due to the city's location – it sits in a high "bowl", surrounded by mountains. The ozone count exceeds the lax Mexican safety levels on some 300 days a year and the dry season is the worst. Ninety per cent of respiratory infections and illnesses originate from air pollution. The installation of slot machines to dispense oxygen to those desperate for clean air is a pathetic bid to counter the problem.

"In Hungary, the government attributes one in 17 deaths to air pollution. In Bombay breathing the air is equivalent to smoking 10 cigarettes a day. And in Beijing air pollution-related respiratory disease is so common that it has been dubbed the 'Beijing cough'".

Hilary French, Worldwatch, 1990

Factory smoke in Mexico City
A cement factory (right) sited in Mexico City, typical of the many industries fouling the air with unacceptable levels of pollution. In 1990 unprecedented levels in the city actually prompted a 30% temporary compulsory reduction of industrial output.

Health hazard for people and plants

Urban air pollution is a major contributory factor to bad health in cities and it has serious effects on plant health too. During warm, sunny weather combustion gases such as nitrogen oxides react with hydrocarbons, causing great clouds of noxious haze to cover cities. A major ingredient in this is ozone, which damages lung tissue and also eats in to plant leaf tissue. In the hot summer of 1988 New York exceeded the federal health standard on 34 days: in Los Angeles on no less than 172 days. In the vicinity of large cities such as Los Angeles and Zurich, the high ozone concentrations cause substantial crop damage.

government surveys indicate forest damage exceeding 50 per cent: air pollution from cities is the main culprit. A noxious cocktail of sulphur dioxides, nitrogen oxides (NOx), and thousands of new trace gases from our urban industries contribute to this pollution and to its byproduct, acid rain. Another byproduct is low-level ozone, which has a highly corrosive effect on vegetation. In large areas of the USA, Canada, India, Brazil, and Mexico, where large quantities of coal and oil are burned, trees are significantly damaged. They lose leaves or needles and suffer distortion of their branching patterns. Diminished growth results in conifers where needle loss exceeds 25 per cent. Air pollution weakens trees' resistance to disease, and so contributes to the ever-greater incidence of fungal diseases affecting them.

In Europe tree damage is causing an annual loss of timber estimated at $29 billion a year. Eighty per cent of conifer forests and 40 per cent of broadleaf forests are receiving excessive air pollution. In eastern Europe there is an annual timber harvest loss of 70 million cubic metres, compared with 48 million in the rest of Europe due to air pollution.

NOx and acid rain

While sulphur dioxide released by cities is actually going down in developed countries due to curbs being implemented – nitrogen oxide (NOx) outputs, generated mainly by oil combustion, are still on the increase. These are produced by high-temperature burning in power station furnaces, and also in petrol and diesel engines. The nitrogen in the air reacts with oxygen during combustion and produces NOx. This was blown out of the chimney or exhaust pipe and has an effect on vegetation and soils similar to sulphur dioxide. In gaseous form, NOx causes damage to plant tissues; in the presence of moisture it turns into nitric acid, and is a major constituent of acid mist or rain. NOx emissions in Europe, according to the government-sponsored European Monitoring and Evaluation Programme, have actually increased by one million tonnes between 1985 and 1988, from 19.5 to 20.5 million tonnes.

Lungs and trees
Dead trees and stumps because of pollution in Recklinghausen, Germany (main picture). False colour arteriograph of a lung (left).

Why global warming?

City dwellers of the rich, industrial nations, with their cars, centrally heated homes, and their mass consumption of processed foods, burn the bulk of the Earth's fossil fuels. This massive combustion results in the release of waste gases and it is these gases, such as carbon dioxide (CO_2), nitrous oxides, methane, and CFCs that cause global warming. They trap solar radiation in the atmosphere, which then causes a rise in temperature. CO_2 in the atmosphere has increased by 25 per cent in the last hundred years. Most scientists agree that global warming is a reality, since mean temperatures have gone up by 0.5°C since the Industrial Revolution, and the hottest years ever recorded were during the 1980s and 1990s.

Changing sea levels

A sea level rise of 15cm has already occurred over the past hundred years. If the Arctic ice cap melts due to global warming and if expansion of water continues, the most extreme forecast is that global sea levels could rise one metre by the middle of the 21st century. A rise of this magnitude could result in the world map changing shape; regions such as Florida and Bangladesh could shrink. And, there could be 50 million environmental refugees, since one-third of the world's population live within 65km of the sea.

Defences for the rich, flooding for the poor

Protective defences from the rising sea would be hugely expensive; the construction of coastal barriers would cost trillions. Wealthy countries are likely to make the investment to protect valuable coastal real estate, but poor ones such as Vietnam, Bangladesh, and Mozambique would be unable to afford dykes.

The last chance

It is not too late to counter global warming if stringent measures are taken for energy efficiency. Massive tree planting schemes are essential; reforestation of one million square kilometres could absorb one billion tonnes of CO_2.

Cities drowning the world

Many of the world's cities have coastal locations. New York, Los Angeles, Miami, Rio de Janeiro, London, Amsterdam, Venice, Bombay, Alexandria, Dhaka, Shanghai, Hong Kong, and Sydney could all be seriously affected by sea level rises. Their food supply would be threatened as a result of increased droughts and a northward shift of agricultural belts and coastal farmland could be affected by salinization and flooding. Thus cities are both victim and cause of sea level rises.

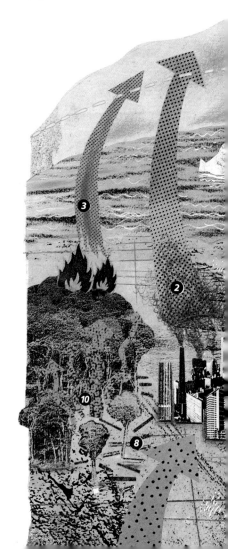

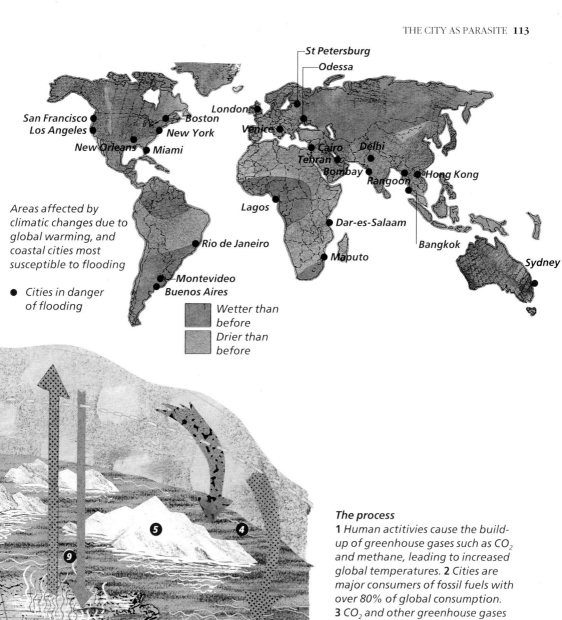

St Petersburg
Odessa
London
Venice
San Francisco
Los Angeles
New Orleans
Boston
New York
Miami
Cairo
Delhi
Tehran
Bombay
Rangoon
Hong Kong
Lagos
Dar-es-Salaam
Bangkok
Rio de Janeiro
Maputo
Sydney
Montevideo
Buenos Aires

Areas affected by climatic changes due to global warming, and coastal cities most susceptible to flooding

● Cities in danger of flooding

Wetter than before

Drier than before

The process
1 Human actitivies cause the build-up of greenhouse gases such as CO_2 and methane, leading to increased global temperatures. **2** Cities are major consumers of fossil fuels with over 80% of global consumption. **3** CO_2 and other greenhouse gases are released from the large scale burning of forests. **4** Sea water warms and expands. **5** Glaciers and ice caps melt. **6** Sea levels rise and drown coastal cities and land. **7** Environmental refugees move inland. **8** Increased demand of cities for food and timber causes tropical deforestation, further adding to global warming. **9** Increasing global temperatures may melt the permafrost, which releases methane, a greenhouse gas 25 times more potent than CO_2. **10** Drying of the tropics and land denudation reduces agricultural potential.

Cities of death

Disaster areas

Many cities of the former Soviet Union and eastern Europe are environmental write-offs – mainly caused by ruthless industrial production without regard to environmental consequences. The legacy is reflected in the new official statistics – 16 per cent of the territory of the former Soviet Union, now the Commonwealth of Independent States (CIS), is considered a disaster area. The health costs of pollution are estimated at 11 per cent of the GNP. Before the break-up of the republic, air pollution in 103 cities, with 50 million inhabitants, exceeded the official standards by 10 times. One hundred billion roubles would be needed to reduce air pollution to acceptable levels.

Bitterfeld – a bitter legacy

The town of Bitterfeld in eastern Germany, after decades of chemical production, has a terrible legacy of pollution, one of the worst in the world. Before Reunification the chimneys of hundreds of factories producing pesticides, plastics, and fertilizers belched out multi-coloured smoke. The River Mulde, so severely polluted, was biologically dead. The town was the centrepiece of a chemical industry, which at its height, employed nearly 350,000 people, producing 20 per cent of the GNP of the GDR. The smoke in the sky seemed to be a sign of industrial success, but Bitterfeld became a toxic wasteland, where simply breathing was life-threatening. Most of the factories and production plants have now been closed down.

Concrete jungle

Accompanying rampant industrialization are the ugly and unsafe concrete apartment blocks that are common to all CIS and eastern European cities. Tens of thousands have been constructed and they will be one of the most enduring legacies of the old Soviet system. But shoddy construction means they cannot stand up to the harsh climatic conditions, and they have already started to decay.

In the industrial centres of Poland, Czechoslovakia, Bulgaria, Hungary, Romania, and what was East Germany life expectancy is about five years lower than in "cleaner" areas. In Poland's industrial upper Silesia circulatory problems are 155% above the national standard; there are 30% more cancers, and 47% more respiratory diseases. Factories emitting lead, cadmium, arsenic, chlorinated hydrocarbons, and radioactive compounds are the norm. And so are the associated health problems: reduced immunity, ulcers, bronchial disease, cranial infections, congenital birth defects, lung cancer, and leukaemia are all commonplace.

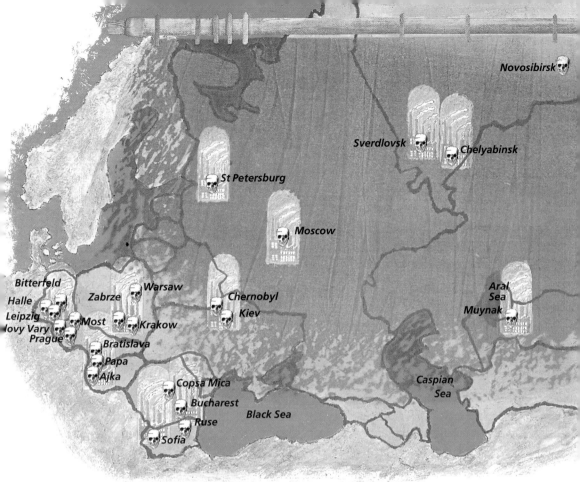

Novosibirsk

Sverdlovsk   Chelyabinsk

St Petersburg

Moscow

Bitterfeld   Warsaw
Halle   Zabrze   Chernobyl   Aral
Leipzig   Kiev   Sea
Jovy Vary   Most   Krakow   Muynak
Prague
Bratislava
Papa
Ajka   Copsa Mica   Caspian
Sofia   Bucharest   Sea
Ruse   Black Sea

Behind the curtain
The lifting of the Iron Curtain revealed horrendous pollution problems. Industrial cities, "hidden" from the west, have to cope with a legacy of environmental devastation.

"We have laid waste to our soil and the rivers and the forests that our forefathers bequeathed to us, and today we have the worst environment in the whole of Europe."

Vaclav Havel, president of Czechoslovakia, 1990

Copsa Mica, Romania
A worker leaving his factory after a non-stop shift.

Healing the city

As cities fast become humanity's premier habitat the challenge of the future is to give people a sense of existential security. Cities must become socially, economically, and ecologically sustainable, fulfilling basic human needs for shelter, subsistence, and social cohesion. For this to work the active participation of people in shaping their urban environment is crucial. But the challenge today goes beyond this. We need to understand the impact of our urban lifestyle on the planet, our home. We must take responsibility for creating an urban lifestyle that is compatible with sustaining an intact biosphere and all its living species. There is no one city that can serve as a model for what we have to achieve. But we can piece together examples from all over the world to show us what needs to be done, and what can be done.

"We are moving into the unknown. We do not know how man is going to express himself, but this is no reason why we should not build the proper frame round him. Otherwise, we shall be heading towards anarchy."

Arnold Toynbee, *Cities of Destiny*

CHAPTER 5

Real people, real cities

Civilization not mobilization
People the world over need lively, imaginative, secure places in which to live, to work, and to relax. For cities to be healthy, attractive, and prosperous, significant changes must happen and the many initiatives that have already started worldwide must come to fruition. Cities must remind themselves that they are centres of excellence, of civilization, rather than temporary camps for the mobilization of people in a motorized, ever-restless quest for the unobtainable.

Cities coming to life
The revival of city centres and their neighbourhoods, the cultural and social heartland that is so often allowed to fall into decay, is crucial in the bid to bring cities back to life (see pp. 120-1). Urban living at its best is a reflection of the human mind's capacity for quirky, joyful creativity, and celebration of city life. Street festivals and carnivals (see pp. 126-7) are enjoying a revival, allowing people to express these things, and to transcend the straitjacket of cold materialism.

People know their own needs
Real cities are made by the people who live in them, not by remote bureaucracies; people are perfectly capable of articulating their needs and have the skills to fulfil them. Real communities, too, can only be created by their inhabitants; they cannot be made artificially. Cities in the developing world, in particular, show that in the face of extraordinary adversity people are able to find solutions to the problems they face. Many examples prove that where self-determination replaces unresponsive authority, people improve their circumstances come what may, particularly in housing. Many cities lack sufficient funds for adequate housing and so allowing people to build their own homes (see pp. 128-31) and upgrade them gradually from modest beginnings is a good solution and has often proved to be money well spent. Residents want to make their own contributions to shaping their environment, and allowing them to do so is a crucial step in improving urban living conditions.

The convivial city

It is a great art to make a city convivial, as the best examples we have inherited show us. Cities such as Florence, Salzburg, and Prague seem to have been purpose-built for lively interchanges between people. Narrow, human-scale streets contrast with well-appointed public buildings and wide, open gathering spaces. They are products of good planning but also of organic growth; they are functional but remain on a human scale; they are centres of economic activity but also of social and cultural energy.

"... the most important resource for the future city ... is the knowledge, ingenuity, and organizational capacity of citizens themselves".

Jorge Hardoy and David Satterthwaite, *The Poor Die Young*

"Stadtluft macht frei – city air makes you free."

German proverb, anon, Middle Ages

The city memory

The urban centre is a city's memory cast in brick and stone. This is where the city starts its long journey into the future, and its gradual expansion into the local countryside. The steps along the way are recorded in the design of buildings, the layout of streets and public places, all permanently imprinted in people's minds. Cities change slowly over time, but cathedrals, mosques, temples, and market squares retain their magnetic function over generations. Urban centres define the character of cities better than anything else. Their museums, theatres, and concert halls provide a context in which past cultural achievements are brought into the present and measured against contemporary accomplishments. Most large cities are also centres of learning, transmitting accumulated knowledge on which future achievements can be built.

Money versus people

The inner city, once a populated place where local people lived, worked, courted, and worshipped, has become a place where money is made, and in recent years the interests of capital have increasingly come into conflict with the concerns of people. Often housing has given way to office blocks as valuable inner-city land became "ripe for development". Markets and workshop spaces were removed to make way for offices and banks. People and old buildings had to give way. In many a city centre the old heart and the architectural memory has been torn out, sacrificed to money, as system-building came to replace hand-crafted construction. Shopping centres and office blocks sprang up instead of mixed-use buildings; multi-lane motorways took the place of streets designed for horse and cart and human feet. As multi-storey blocks increasingly towered over churches and market halls, urban centres became inhospitable places. With people forced to move elsewhere, many "redeveloped" city centres have become windswept wastelands after office hours.

The city heart

The city centre should be the heart of the city. In many cases, it may no longer have a local population, but it can be a centre of workshops, markets, cafés, and dance halls, which continue to provide for rituals of free association between

Block 103, Berlin Kreuzberg

In the Berlin district of Kreuzberg a remarkable urban renewal project has come to fruition, a collaboration between the local German and Turkish communities and STERN, a local architects' practice led by Peter Beck. Twenty-five run-down tenement buildings with 800 residents have been comprehensively refurbished to create a socially and ecologically satisfactory neighbourhood. A programme of house insulation was set up in conjunction with a combined heat and power system for the whole block. Yards and roofs have been planted with vegetation, rainwater collection and filtration systems have been installed. On some house roofs photo-voltaic panels have been put in place. The project has established "eco-standards" for public housing refurbishment throughout Berlin.

"Every ugly or senseless building is an insult to the man passing in front of it. Every building should be embellished and adding to its culture. This is very difficult now that we have abandoned human scale and 'human reference'. We need to reintroduce human scale, human reference and musicality into architecture."

Dr Hassan Fathy, Egyptian architect

People's Association, Notting Hill, London

The early 1970s was the age of the "people's association". Increasingly people realized that they had a right, and a duty, to participate in the shaping of their community. Planners and architects had behaved like dictators long enough. In the London district of Notting Hill Gate few children had play space and were forced to use the streets. As motor traffic increased, so did accidents. When two children were run over in quick succession the local community decided to take over an area of derelict land belonging to a property developer and turn it into a neighbourhood park. A people's association proceeded to take over derelict houses and transform them into a café, nursery, and training workshops. A new spirit of community self-determination had been born.

"A riot makes a much greater impact on government thinking than any amount of earnest and accurate research."

D. Donnison

"It is time for more experiments in the way we plan, build and own our communities. For example, new initiatives are needed to try and find ways to ensure that our surroundings are not entirely sacrificed to the car."

Prince Charles, *A Vision of Britain*, 1989

people. City centres are melting pots that continuously merge together human experiences and creativity. And they should be centres of inter-cultural communication, where people from different traditions can learn about, and from, each other. This cultural exchange is important in a world in which global communications are increasingly taken for granted. Urban cultural diversity can cause tensions and clashes, but it also gives rise to pluralism and tolerance. It is crucial for the future of cities that this pluralism is not stifled, but actively encouraged. Today's cities are world cities – for better or worse. They have to provide models for how people can learn to live together in an increasingly interdependent world.

Crisis and opportunity

All over the developed world powerful centrifugal forces have been at work, dispelling people from inner cities to the periphery. Many half-empty city centres have become the abode of social problems. Run-down tenement buildings, often abandoned by their former residents, who preferred the greater safety of the suburbs (see also pp. 58-9), have been taken over by the socially disadvantaged. Many major cities such as Washington, New York, Los Angeles, London, Birmingham, Liverpool, Zurich, and Marseilles have experienced growing confrontations between minority groups and the police.

But the human and architectural alienation of city centres has also been a source of cultural revival. Inner-city riots, resulting from unemployment and bad housing conditions, have often served to concentrate the minds of governments wonderfully. Protest about inhuman cities has turned into creativity; anger about bad housing conditions has brought about inner-city housing initiatives. Urban authorities have also been forced to realize that people have their own contributions to make to urban planning and redesign. In cities such as London, Berlin, and New York neighbourhood action groups have had a major input into the design of urban centres and inner-city neighbourhoods.

Footloose money

Market economies with a high turnover invariably generate high cashflows. Most goods and services that are used in modern cities originate elsewhere, fulfilling urban needs without concern for the effects on local economies. The money used for transactions is usually footloose; much of it flows back to the company that produced and sold the goods in the first place, often based in a far-away place. Money is a global commodity and a means of exchange and it is always attracted to places that earn a high rate of return. It has little concern for the stability and cohesion of communities and less "attractive" places often lose out.

Money earned in local communities drains out into the world economy without much local benefit, weakening the local economic base and causing local economies to suffer chronic cash haemor-rhages. Poor areas of the world, suppliers of raw materials and foodstuffs to richer countries, suffer disproportionately; as value is added the rich get richer and the poor get poorer.

The communal merry-go-round
Traditional communities usually operated on mutual aid principles. Carpenters, potters, and weavers would often barter their services with little money changing hands. People helped each other build houses and harvest crops. Since few goods had to be brought in from outside the area, little money was actually needed to supply and service the community.

The need for cash
The industrial market economy has steadily increased people's need for cash earnings. In the "official" economy money, not people, has taken centre stage. The resulting cashflow through the economy mirrors our use of goods and services; we purchase them with few concerns about the local effects of our spending patterns.

Local Employment Trading System (LETS)
In order to keep the benefits of our spending power in the community, it is necessary to develop a local means of exchange; a local currency that does not "leak" into the wider economy. A new system of barter has been developed in Canada called LETS (see above right). It is designed to help people with little money to expand their economic activity.

How LETS works

LETS is a computerized local register of goods and services, matching supply and demand for the benefit of local people. Individuals and businesses can become involved in this modern barter arrangement in which transactions take place without cash exchanging hands and leaving the community. Whoever supplies the goods or services has their name and the value of the transaction registered and is credited to that extent, while the recipient owes services to the system. General-ized reciprocity, with the accumu-lation of debits and credits, benefits the whole community far more than the modern through-put economic system based on money.

LETS in Stroud, England
The English country town Stroud has a LETS scheme, which uses the "Stroud" as a monetary substitute. Members use special cheque books to pay for a wide variety of services, from bicycle repairs to holistic psy-chotherapy. Administrators collect the cheques and update a computer log of transactions. Trust and trust-worthiness are important to the health of the system, but there is a mechanism for coping with bad debts, if they should occur. They would be divided up equally between the other members.

Through-put
In the existing economic system (top left) money enters the community from an external source, passes between individuals as goods and services are purchased, and is eventually lost to the outside again.

"The whole system is founded on trust. Without it there would be no LETS. We have no credit control as such – we just trust each other."

"It's just a marvellous, marvellous idea. It may sound strange, it may even sound cranky. What is important is that it works."

Jo, Stroud LETS

Self-help
In a trading system without money (bottom left), skills are bartered and exchanged and little money needs to be used. Resources are kept within the community, so local people are able to continue benefitting from them; even those without money can participate in the local economy.

A town within a town

Let the wild flowers grow

All over the developed world there has always been a minority of people who feel strongly that our urban-industrial world is deficient in many ways; they reject the rat race, the dependence on non-renewable resources, the all-pervading materialism and the fragmentation of society. These "outsiders", who find it hard to make a living conventionally or to integrate with society, often become squatters, taking over empty buildings in a city to make a temporary home. Many squatters seek out a communal lifestyle to create a new family, a "family of choice", formed with people who have shared interests. Such people may not fit into the ready-made categories and rule books of society, but they formulate their own rules, and by doing so help society to broaden its outlook.

Free town, Christiania

In the centre of Copenhagen, in a park on the edge of a lake, a communal experiment has been going on since 1971 – "the free town of Christiania". A former army camp, Christiania became an extraordinary experiment in a very conservative country. It attracted people who were disenchanted with society; often people with great creativity and imagination. It soon developed into a community of around 1000 people, a self-styled free town "in the tradition of Europe's medieval free towns". Before long the town had its own baker, candle maker, blacksmith, potters, weavers, and many other craft workers.

Visitor-ambassadors

Christiania soon had floods of visitors who participated in its communal life for a few days or weeks a year and who became its ambassadors in the outside world. The presence of this large support group made it hard for successive Danish governments to close down the "anarchist" town. Christiania today has all the strengths and weaknesses of a 1960s-style community: it can be self-indulgent – a social experiment that thinks it might change the world. Despite many problems, it stands firm as a truly caring community.

The Danish government has increasingly come to respect the fact that Christiania looks after and integrates people who find "ordinary" society difficult, in a "cost-effective" way. The town exists in conflict, but also in symbiosis with, Danish society. And it does so by utilizing alternative social structures and forms of social organization. The community is run as a neighbourhood democracy, without a "head" person. Local meetings deal with any conflicts and new initiatives.

"The aim of Christiania is the development of an autonomous society in which each individual can evolve freely, but remains responsible to the community as a whole. The society should be economically independent; the shared aim must always be that we should try and show that it is possible to prevent the spiritual and physical environmental pollution of people."

Declaration, November 1971

"There is not enough work in Denmark, so the people who don't want to work can be unemployed and live in Christiania where they can learn about not working or they can work on things which interest them, and the way in which they do so – although perhaps not geared to market requirements – is nonetheless in human terms very fulfilling." Christiania resident

The last twenty years
Since its foundation 20 years ago, Christiania has gradually been changing from a community on the fringes of Danish society (right), to just another district of Copenhagen (above).

Celebration, pride, and identity

Street festivals and carnivals are important for the social wellbeing of cities. As people decorate their streets with garlands and balloons they project a pride of place on their shared home. Since urban neighbourhoods consist of people who often come from very different places and backgrounds, street festivals are important for social cohesion, bringing people together in celebration and laughter. It is often during street parties that people living in close proximity actually meet and talk to one another for the first time. That way conflicts can be resolved and neighbourhood actions can be developed and brought to fruition to benefit all.

Carnival time in European cities

In Europe carnival goes back to pagan times, as the often grotesque masks worn in some traditional festivals in German and Spanish towns still show. Across Europe carnival is celebrated mainly in Catholic cities during the cold, grey days of winter when the human spirit is most in need of colour, music, and excitement. It fills the city streets with fancy dress processions, the sounds of drums, and the pipes of Pan. Carnival is a time of letting go, of exuberance before the six weeks of fasting prescribed by the Christian calendar in the run-up to Easter.

Notting Hill Carnival, London

In London carnival is a summer event. Begun in 1967, when a social worker decided that a carnival would help to bring together people from disparate ethnic and social backgrounds, it became an annual event that has grown from small beginnings to become a national event, which now draws millions of people. Today the festivities are organized by the black community and floats carry Trinidadian steel bands and loudspeaker systems playing the latest reggae and calypso music. For years the carnival was marred by confrontations between revellers and the police, but better tactics and organization have greatly reduced the level of conflict. A marginal activity has turned into a major annual event now copied throughout Britain, bringing colour and fun into dreary city streets.

The samba schools, Rio de Janeiro

The *escolas de samba*, who organize the extravagantly decorated floats, mainly originate in the shanties on the hills around the city. Detailed planning, which takes all year, involves selecting a theme which is echoed in a specially written song, the *samba-enredo*, the costumes, and the floats. Each school has an organizer, the *carnavalesco*, who orchestrates the event. Judging is based on ten aspects of presentation

and the best school wins the title
campea do carnaval, champion
of the carnival, which carries the
ultimate kudos.

The craziest carnival
*First started in 1852, the
Rio carnival (below) is now
world-famous. For four
days in February thousands
of people block the streets
following their favourite
bandas – musicians and
dancers dressed in exuber-
ant fantasias.*

Activity of hope

Squatting – the only option

In developing-world countries there are few dwellings for the millions of people who arrive every year from the provinces (see pp. 70-1), on top of the ever-increasing number of new families formed in the city. Most people cannot afford to buy or rent even the cheapest homes on the market. Few bother to apply for the tiny number of subsidized homes. Low-income families depend on the squatter settlements that surround most developing-world cities. Illegal building is the rule and in the past a typical response of urban authorities has been to send in police and bulldozers.

Gradual upgrading

What most critics did not appreciate is that squatter settlements need not necessarily be places of squalor. Given half a chance, people will upgrade their cardboard houses into ones made from wood or corrugated iron. Given sufficient funds and security of land tenure, they will gradually build solid brick houses, which they enlarge as their families grow and their financial situations improve. In this way squatter settlements gradually turn into "respectable" neighbourhoods, full of homes to be proud of. And the construction work generates much-needed employment.

Gradual change of opinion

For many years urban authorities resisted spontaneous urban development, yet did not offer viable alternatives. At last it is being recognized that bulldozers are not solving anything and that self-help housing by squatters is a realistic solution that should be supported. Self-help communities are not usually able to operate efficiently without outside support, but urban authorities willing to organize road links, water supply, sewage systems, and electricity are still a rarity. However, in recent years there has been a gradual change of opinion in favour of support for self-help communities.

Villa el Salvador, Lima

One of the largest settlements in the world built by a self-help housing co-operative was Villa el Salva-

In most developing-world cities between half and three-quarters of new homes are built by low-income people themselves, who show resourcefulness and economy rare in the throw-away developed world. Indeed they have to. Typically they manage to build five times as much for the same money as governments or local authorities do. Self-determination and mutual aid are the critical factors: people know their own needs and what they can accomplish with available resources. In time people upgrade houses, providing they can be sure of security of tenure. Support of mutual neighbourhood aid is the key for stable urban communities.

"We . . . are committed to reversing current trends towards ever-increasing homelessness, overcrowding, lack of basic services, and other forms of . . . depravation. . . . Poverty is our constant emergency. Adequate, affordable shelter with basic services is a right of all people. . . . Worldwide, it is low-income people who are responsible for the planning and construction of most new houses. . . . Government should recognize that appropriate support for individual households and community-based organizations that they form . . . represents the most innovative and effective strategy to reverse existing trends. . . ."

Excerpt from the 1987 Limuru Declaration of 57 non-governmental organizations from around the world, addressing the world's housing problems

Reaching down
Authorities have resources and power: facilitating self-help is an efficient way to use these.

Sewage

Roads

Water

Work

Power

Materials

Somewhere to live

Self-esteem

Co-operative working

Identity

Local control

Reaching up
With appropriate support self-help community builders are capable of transforming the housing crisis in developing-world cities.

dor. Over 200,000 low-income people live in this "pueblo joven", young town, of more than 30,000 houses, which grew out of desert sand in the early 1970s. Today the landscape is covered with trees and gardens – the desert has turned green.

The self-managed Community of Villa el Salvador (CUAVES) illustrates vividly that self-build housing and self-government can be made to work. Starting with the occupation of government-owned land by poor people in 1971 the improvised settlement grew to 20,000 households in a matter of months. Lima's cash-strapped city authority realized the cost-effectiveness of the self-help approach to housing, and with its support the community grew rapidly. For some years, the Peruvian government also helped with site planning and infrastructure development. But it was, above all, the initiative and investment by its people that made the community a reality. Today Villa El Salvador has its own municipal authority, which is able to take measures to improve roads, drinking water and electricity supplies, plant trees, and improve community facilities.

Klong Toey, Bangkok

With over 40,000 people Klong Toey is Bangkok's largest squatter camp. Long held up as an unacceptable example of urban squalor, Bangkok's authorities tried many times to get rid of the people and their houses. But this resilient community, after years of struggle, had learned to negotiate. In 1982, after many conflicts, an agreement was reached with the Port Authority of Thailand, giving the people a 20-year lease for part of the land they occupied. The land-sharing arrangement between authority and community has resulted in an end to evictions. Thailand's National Housing Authority helped local people's organizations to build and improve thousands of homes, to relocate others, and to organize proper services for the community. With a securer future people have been able to get on with improving their houses and their lives.

Resourcefulness and determination

"When we see great numbers of low-income people building and improving their communities, and at costs three or five times lower than those built for them, we must admit that we have a great deal to learn from those builders and their enablers."

John F. C. Turner, *Building Community*, 1988

"Where dwellers control the major decisions and are free to make their own contributions in the design, construction or management of their housing, both this process and the environment produced stimulate individual and social well-being. When people have no control over nor responsibility for key *decisions in the housing process, on the other hand, dwelling environments may instead become a barrier to personal fulfillment and a burden on the economy."*

John F.C. Turner, *Freedom to Build,* 1972

Steps on the self-help ladder
A house (main picture) near a Santa Fe refuse dump in Mexico City. Typical of first homes built by migrants, it will be progressively improved. The inset shows a street in the Palo Alto housing co-operative.

CHAPTER 6

The inner workings

Health in cities

Cities cannot fulfil their vital functions if they fail to provide a healthy environment for their inhabitants. Human health (see pp. 134-5) depends on a varied and fulfilling lifestyle and increasingly, urban areas are being designed with "health expectancy" in mind. The participation of citizens in projects to create green spaces, minimize noise levels, and provide good housing and secure surroundings tends to produce the best results. Such healthy environments mean that urban populations are not forced to take refuge in green spaces beyond the city gates.

Greening the urban environment

Inner-city vegetation has advantages in addition to the cosmetic (see pp. 136-41): it absorbs rainfall and prevents flooding; reduces noise levels; and acts as "used air" filters. Green spaces can also add to the urban food supply; today the cultivation of fruit and nut trees in urban areas is topical again. In developing-world cities urban food forests are being introduced, relevant once more because they require little maintenance, allow for play space, and can be highly productive.

Energy sustainability

Modern cities can greatly reduce their need for non-renewable energy supplies by improving their efficiency and by introducing natural energy systems (see pp. 142-5). To make cities sustainable we need to rationalize our transport systems (see pp. 146-51). The motor car has given greater freedom to some people, but has reduced that of many others because streets have become more dangerous and public services have been cut. Fuel efficiency has been vastly improved where efficient public transport systems operate.

Recycling city

Recycling waste (see pp. 152-5) can enhance the resource efficiency of cities, bringing them economic as well as environmental benefits. In the long term resource-efficient cities have the competitive edge over those that continue to discard waste.

Revealing the way forward

No two cities are the same. All have their own distinct histories, layout, and topography. Therefore all require different approaches to improve their environmental performances. As urban populations grow worldwide it is vital to organize cities with resource efficiency uppermost in our minds. The functioning of cities depends greatly on the technological systems in use. Trams are making a comeback in many cities where traffic gridlock and air pollution have forced urban authorities to reassess their transport policies. Energy-efficient buildings are

The city splits
An interconnecting range (right) of "green" alternatives is already in place in many cities, waiting to be used.

revolutionizing urban design. Solar and wind power are becoming mainstream technologies as air pollution and the fear of nuclear disasters are forcing a rethink. Sustainable urban living will determine the future of our cities.

Health promotion

One of the most important purposes of the organization of urban life is to provide city residents with healthy living environments. Good cities practise "health promotion", encouraging people to lead healthy, purposeful lives. To achieve this requires not just medical doctors; it assumes the collaboration of the whole community.

Unhealthy lifestyle

The human body evolved to suit the environment and way of life of our distant hunter-gatherer ancestors. They breathed clean air, travelled on foot, lived in close-knit communities, and ate a natural, varied diet. Today we breathe polluted air, move about less, are often isolated, and eat mostly processed food. The urban environment is an artificial one and without careful manipulation it can cause chronic disease and a profound lack of wellbeing.

The "human monoculture"

The combination of sedentary urban living and stressful lifestyles result in a range of health problems, from bronchitis and asthma, back trouble, psychological problems, and stress-related heart disease, to digestive disorders and obesity. The "human monoculture" of cities enables the ready transmission of bacterial and viral infections. While the occurrence of previously common diseases such as cholera, malaria, dysentery, and tuberculosis has been reduced in developed cities by modern sanitation, pesticides, and antibiotics, these diseases still persist in developing-world cities lacking such benefits.

In many cities people are exposed to environmental toxins that cause ill health (see pp. 114-15), and health problems in developed-world cities are tackled primarily by curative care. But in some countries new preventative approaches are gaining ground, designed not only to keep the individual healthy but also to create healthy living and environmental conditions.

Healthy cities programmes

The city of Toronto was one of the first to pursue the concept of the "healthy city". In 1979 the city established a Health Advocacy Unit, undertaking a community health survey and soon afterwards establishing the first city Environmental Protection

"A community is like an organism. If any part of the organism isn't working, is ill or diseased, it affects the whole. In a human being a cancerous liver affects the total health of the person. The community is similar."

Professor Leonard Duhl, University of Berkeley, California

"If cities, and indeed nations, are to achieve health for all, they must first look to reducing inequities in the health of their citizens."

Dr Trevor Hancock, Toronto

"Health depends on the human capacity to shape the physical environment in ways which safeguard and promote health and to draw on natural resources in ways which do not threaten the integrity of natural systems on which a stable climate and a sustainable supply of natural resources depend."

David Satterthwaite, IIED, London

Office. Following a conference on urban health in 1984 the city authorities declared that by the year 2000 Toronto would be the healthiest city in North America. The intention was not just to provide adequate medical care for its citizens, maximizing their life expectancy, but to create the conditions for people to enjoy a healthy way of life *and* maximize their life expectancy too.

The city's Department of Public Health today encourages personal skills for health and offers advice about preventative options. This initiative has since been adopted by international bodies such as the World Health Organisation whose Healthy Cities Programme is trying to shift the emphasis of health care to the provision of urban environmental conditions conducive to good health. Five hundred cities in many countries are now pursuing "healthy city" ideas.

Health in developing-world cities

Cities in the developing world are suffering many of the health problems that afflicted European cities in the nineteenth century. Lack of sanitation, bad drinking water, air pollution, malnutrition, crowding, and bad housing are commonplace. Exposure to pathogens and pollutants is a constant threat and intestinal infections and respiratory diseases are major causes of ill health. Modern disinfectants and medicines are essential for the survival of millions, but in many instances are too expensive for the majority of the world's poor.

Child-to-Child scheme, Bombay

All developing-world cities have some health-care facilities, though poor residents have less access to them. In many places voluntary groups have established community health care schemes to counter this. In a Bombay shanty town of 100,000 inhabitants living in tin shacks with no sanitation, Dr Vijayar Bhalerao has developed a programme to train children as health workers. The Child-to-Child scheme involves children as young as ten who are trained to look after the health care needs of other children. They diagnose diseases and prescribe basic remedies with the professionalism of real doctors: only when they cannot be certain about diagnosing or treating a complaint do they ask a doctor for help. The lives of many children in the community have been saved by these young workers.

The Ottawa Charter of Health Promotion

Strategies for health promotion:
● Build public health policy
● Create supportive environments
● Strengthen community action
● Develop personal skills
● Reorient health services

Healthy city concepts

A healthy city must:
● Provide a clean and quiet environment
● Be free from pollution and toxins
● Allow freedom of movement
● Provide stimuli to the senses
● Minimize stress for normal living conditions
● Provide easy access to green spaces
● Have conditions for supportive neighbourhoods
● Minimize conditions of individual insecurity

Out of a natural landscape

People are born nature's children, yet cities, our principal habitat, are highly unnatural assemblies of brick, concrete, and steel. All cities have grown out of the natural landscape of rivers, forests, and fields; habitats for a huge variety of life. "Civilization" implies taming nature for human purposes, and throughout the history of cities, nature has, at best, been an afterthought. Medieval cities (see also pp. 44-5) had gardens, but they were for growing food, not for encouraging wilderness. For people to experience the natural world, they had to go beyond the city walls.

Urban parks and gardens

The early 19th century saw the creation of the first public parks. In Britain in 1840 the House of Commons Select Committee on the Health of Towns recognized parks as instruments of social health: they were places for people to relax. People with access to parks would be less prone to disease, crime, and social discontent. But the visionary designer William Morris yearned for more: he wanted a *greening* of cities. He imagined Trafalgar Square, London, as an apricot orchard and the area around Shaftesbury Avenue as a rose garden. He envisaged much of London returning to woodland. Ebenezer Howard, with his Garden Cities concept (see pp. 54-5), followed Morris's idea of the co-existence of city and country in one place.

The greening of cities

In the last 20 years this thinking has gained many new adherents in the vigorous "green cities" movement, which wants nature to permeate the city, transforming urban landscapes. People started turning wasteland into urban farms and tree-planting became popular again as the environmental value of trees became more apparent. Allotments experienced a revival, new mini-parks tucked away behind rows of houses came to life, and disused rail lines were turned into linear parks, which allowed spaces for people to go for walks and for wildlife to "commute" between the countryside and the inner city. The facades of houses were planted with vines,

Cracks in the concrete

Nature is ever present in the concrete jungle; it is impossible to eradicate it. Left to its own devices, it breaks through weaknesses in road, pavement, or rooftile, asserting its right to exist in a world dominated by urban people.

"What do we mean by urban planting? We mean the restoration, creation and maintenance of plant life in and around cities. This includes parks, median strips, sidewalk and rooftop planting, community and private gardens and vacant lots. It includes shade and fruit trees, vegetable patches, grasslands and scrub or chaparral."

Peter Berg, A Green City Programme

to create shade and contribute to natural house insulation. The concept of "urban permaculture" (long-term crop-growing in the city, see pp. 172-3) became fashionable in countries such as Australia, the USA, and Germany.

Necessity not luxury

The green cities movement does not see nature in the city as an expensive luxury: the presence of vegetation helps reduce pollution, improves rainwater collection, and it provides recreational sites for people, thereby reducing urban stress. Green spaces can also add considerably to the urban food supply, with allotments and urban farms a normal part of people's lives. These farms retain their fertility from urban leaves and lawn clippings that are composted, enriching the soil.

Trees, wonderful trees

Trees are beautiful, but they also provide valuable environmental benefits. They are the planet's air conditioners, but without producing the unwanted waste products. In cities they fulfil the same function: cities without trees are poorer places. A single tree can transpire as much as 380 litres of water a day, cooling the air in the vicinity. They also absorb and filter dust in polluted cities. A 40-cm-diameter Douglas fir can remove 19.5kg of sulphur from the air per year, without injury to itself. Urban forester James Schmidt calculated that 50 million trees, taking up 5 per cent of the urban land area of St Louis, Mississippi, would suffice to clean the 455,000 tonnes of sulphur dioxide emissions from the city. Broadleaf trees are particularly useful because they have ten times the leaf area of the soil on which they stand: a hundred-year-old beech has some 800,000 leaves. Roadside trees give off oxygen during the day and help to reduce both carbon monoxide and dioxide levels along heavy traffic routes. Trees also help to slow down wind gusting through cities.

Ornamental trees or fruit trees?

In many cities fruit trees are an essential part of the urban landscape, both in temperate and tropical areas. Fruit and nut trees, while providing shade

Involving the community

Planting trees, greening urban spaces, and planning land-use changes in general must be done in consultation with local communities. These are the people who know best how spare land in their area might be used. Tree planting, for example, can fail: many a newly planted urban tree has been snapped in two just because it has been planted in the wrong place. Derelict land in the city may already

be in use: children may use it as an adventure playground or travellers may need it for grazing ponies. With the consent of the people greenery for the benefit of all can be accommodated even in densely populated areas.

Tree planting
Children plant trees (below) in the Chalco district of Mexico City, where a major tree-planting scheme is taking place.

and a green ambience, as ornamental trees do, can also contribute substantially to the urban food supply. In Bangalore, India, 25 per cent of trees are fruit trees. The old part of the Amazon town Belém, Brazil, is a grove of huge mango trees, while Stockholm and Prague are both full of apple, plum, and pear trees.

The return of urban farming

Times of scarcity invariably encourage urban farming. In World War II cities in Europe on both sides vastly increased food production as access to the countryside became precarious. Post-war low-energy costs made food from distant places available to cities. It led to a demise in urban farming and vegetable gardening, particularly as concern over lead-contaminated soils grew. Today urban farming thrives in areas of high unemployment.

Ashram Acres, Birmingham

In Birmingham, England, the inner-city area of Sparkbrook is host to an innovative urban land-use project and food-production scheme called Ashram Acres. The project makes use of valuable local skills to utilize derelict gardens in the area, clearing them and making them productive. Another aim is to provide a meeting place for people who vary widely in age, race, and background. High unemployment in the mainly Asian and West Indian community led to an interest in and necessity for the cultivation of vegetable crops – among them specialist crops such as okra, cucumber, karella, and coriander. Animals are also kept, goats providing milk and cheese. Hundreds of people are now involved in the project and derive both therapeutic and economic value from being able to produce fruit and vegetables not normally grown in Britain. "Members" pay a nominal amount to work on the project, and are entitled to take produce home. The vegetables are grown organically in raised compost beds under cheaply made polythene greenhouses, avoiding any contamination by lead in the soil. The huge success of the project has led Birmingham Council to make available to the community a larger one-hectare site outside the city.

Space for people

Dieter Magnus, environmental artist, links art to nature to improve the urban environment, and tries to involve as many collaborators as creatively as possible. His famous pedestrian bridge platform is more than just a means for people to get across a busy road. It is a piece of new urban landscape that tempts, delights, and serves.

"It is an important structure for the residents of the area, it is . . . a perfect example of humane, imaginative architecture. . . . A work of man for real people, who do not just 'use' something, but who at the same time feel, see, hear, smell."

Dr Manfred Sack in the Deutsches Architektenblatt, 1/82

Green Bridge, Mainz *Before the bridge was built (above) pedestrians had to negotiate a dangerous crossing. Now (below) they can stroll uninterrupted between residential and recreational areas.*

Managing urban energy demand

Reducing the urban energy flow is critically important for making cities sustainable. Cities, directly and indirectly, are responsible for the bulk of the planet's energy consumption, with energy flows 100 times higher than in natural ecosystems of similar size. We currently burn up fossil fuels hundreds of thousands of times faster than they are able to accumulate in the Earth's crust. Throughout the world the general public have rejected the nuclear option. So a new approach to urban energy management is crucial if cities are to become sustainable. There are two ways in which this can be done – by improving energy supply systems and by reducing energy consumption.

CHPs: supplying power *and* heat

Many cities could be retrofitted with combined heat and power stations (CHPs), a system particularly suitable for compact districts with high population densities. CHPs generate electricity and produce hot water as a byproduct. This water, which is heated up as it cools the turbines, is piped into homes, factories, public buildings, and swimming pools. Inner-city districts are particularly suitable for CHP because hot water can circulate through the relatively short distances of insulated pipes: cities such as Stockholm, Stuttgart, and Helsinki already operate the system.

City-centre efficiency

CHPs release minimal amounts of polluting gases such as sulphur dioxide (SO_2) and nitrogen oxides (NOx) (see pp. 108-11) by using efficient burners such as "fluidized bed combustion" systems. In addition chimneys can be fitted with scrubbers and catalytic converters to clean the flue gases. CHPs can be located in city centres without fouling up the air, though inevitably their chimneys release some carbon dioxide (CO_2), but this is kept to a minimum due to their great efficiency. Compared with conventional power stations, which are often situated outside cities, inner-city CHP systems are highly effective; a 90-per cent efficiency, compared with about 35 per cent for conventional power plants, is

CHP: the vision that works

Centre-of-town combined heat and power stations are gaining popularity, making eminent sense in the fight against pollution and energy wastage. A town or city that takes responsibility for creating its own efficient energy supply system enables its people to save money and reduce the global impact of energy use at the same time. The city works supply a service to the community and the citizen-shareholders decide whether they want energy at minimal cost or a dividend from profits at the end of the year.

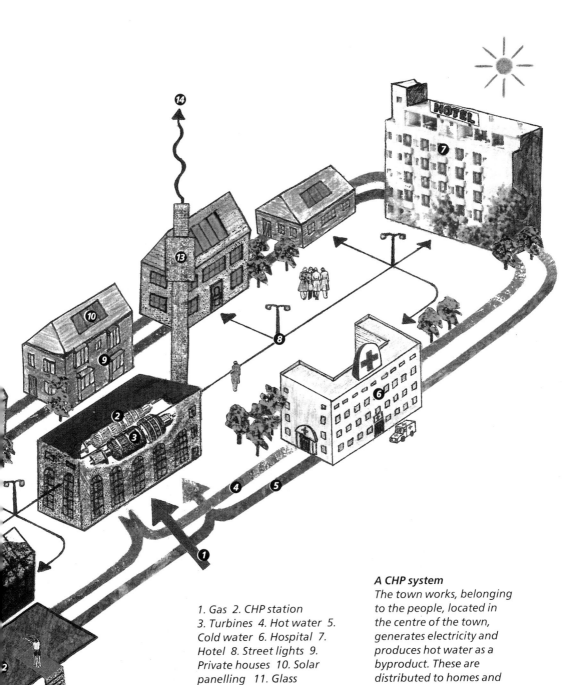

1. Gas 2. CHP station
3. Turbines 4. Hot water 5.
Cold water 6. Hospital 7.
Hotel 8. Street lights 9.
Private houses 10. Solar
panelling 11. Glass
house 12. Swimming
pool 13. Catalytic conver-
ter 14. CO_2

A CHP system
The town works, belonging
to the people, located in
the centre of the town,
generates electricity and
produces hot water as a
byproduct. These are
distributed to homes and
public amenities. Solar
panels top up domestic
heat supplies.

achievable. The electricity travels only a short distance from the power station to the consumer, helping to keep the price of the electricity competitive.

Rottweil, Germany

The small town of Rottweil in Germany has a particularly clever CHP system, among the most efficient in the world. The technology is well matched with its operating system, making it extremely cost-effective and uniquely efficient to operate. Located right in the middle of this picturesque medieval town of 24,000 people, the system uses gas-powered engines to generate three megawatts of electricity. The "waste" heat is pumped around the town, supplying households as well as public buildings and amenities with hot water all year around. Solar collectors tied into the system supply additional hot water when the sun shines, while thermostats and good insulation minimize heat wastage.

The system is operated by the "town works", which is owned by the town people. Since the works is not a profit-oriented enterprise, the incentive to maximize energy throughput has never been present. Rottweil-style CHP systems are now being installed in east German cities, which used to operate some of the most polluting and inefficient power-supply systems in the world, running on acidic lignite coal.

Household energy efficiency

Households consume 30 to 50 per cent of a country's energy, the variations resulting from climate differences as well as varying standards of energy efficiency. House insulation is a key variable in wealthy, hot countries, where air-conditioning swallows a lot of electricity, and in cold ones, which require vast quantities of fuel for heating. A modern office building, efficiently insulated, with identical lighting and heating standards to an older one, typically uses half the electricity. Advanced insulation standards can actually reduce the energy consumption of buildings by as much as 90 per cent. At least 40,000 such buildings existed in the USA in 1992 and 5000 new ones are built every year. In Swedish cities extremely high insulation levels have existed ever since a firewood shortage in the 19th century and loft insulation is often several feet thick. For hot climates improved natural air circulation during the

Energy-efficient appliances

The American energy analyst Amory Lovins is convinced that energy savings in three sectors – lighting, electric motors, and appliances – could reduce our electricity consumption by two-thirds. He has calculated that existing homes in a city such as Austin, Texas, could reduce their electricity consumption by 63%, using available technologies, at a cost of around $2000. Energy savings would be repaid in three years. Better-insulated fridges, cookers, and more efficient electric motors would all play their part.

Photo-voltaics

Photo-voltaic cells that can produce electricity efficiently, even in cloudy conditions, are now becoming competitive in price. In 20 years they have come down from $30 per kilowatt hour to about 30 cents, and by the year 2000 they are expected to be down to 10 cents. They are already being incorporated into the roof construction of houses in the USA. Japanese companies have developed solar-electric roof tiles which could make buildings in cities around the world largely self-sufficient in electricity.

day, can reduce the demand for air-conditioning. In cold countries techniques for storing hot water in the summer for use during the winter have been developed.

The coming solar age

Combustion of coal, gas, and oil still present in the Earth's crust will raise the CO_2 concentration in the atmosphere tenfold, compared with a doubling that has occurred so far (see also pp. 112-13). The use of new, non-polluting energy technologies is therefore critical if our urban lifestyle is to become sustainable. Great strides are now being made to develop economical solar and wind energy systems. It is crucial that such systems should also become available to cities in developing countries, which often use highly polluting energy technology.

Wind power

Windfarms have become lucrative business for farmers with land in windy locations (below).

Solar electricity

California has taken the lead in solar-electricity technology. In the Mojave desert several solar-thermal power stations are producing electricity for Californian cities. They use mirrors to focus the sun's rays on liquid-filled tubes to produce steam for driving generators. Solar power stations each producing some 320 megawatts generate enough electricity for 170,000 people at a competitive 8 cents per kilowatt-hour.

Wind power today

California is also a world-leader in wind power. Enlightened governor Jerry Brown created the legislation to make both solar and wind power feasible options for the state. The wind-power stations of California, several of which have over 10,000 windmills, are giant test beds for a rapidly maturing technology. Each 100 kilowatt windmill costs some $100,000. Wind farms in California produce electricity as cheaply as coal-fired stations and more cheaply than nuclear ones. Many countries have the potential to produce some 20 per cent of their current electricity consumption from wind power.

Transport fuel efficiency and urban density

One hundred people in a bus need only 40 square metres of road space. By contrast, 100 people in cars travelling by themselves need some 2000 square metres. This comparison illustrates a stark reality: cars and their demand for roads have shaped modern cities. Yet cars have not solved people's travel problems, with traffic jams a daily fact of life. New public transport strategies are being tested in cities the world over to reduce car dependence. Greater transport fuel efficiency is an urgent necessity to reduce air pollution and climate change. Urban fuel consumption is a function of layout and built-in travel distances, and of the form of transport used. European and Japanese cities are generally more fuel-efficient than North American ones, both because of denser land use patterns and better public transport. In Tokyo only 15 per cent of commuters drive to work, compared with about 90 per cent in Los Angeles.

Planning for proximity

De-zoning is crucial for reducing commuting distances in cities. It means creating "multi-nucleated" cities with districts accommodating both homes and work places. This is easier in a post-industrial society in which fewer people depend on jobs in large, polluting factories. Planners are also moving toward urban layouts that provide for greater built-in proximity between homes, schools, shops, and places of entertainment and leisure; where civilization based on face-to-face human encounters becomes possible once again. There is a strong revival of the idea of planning cities with much greater density. A major consideration is the distances that people have to travel. In North America, Portland, Oregon, has shown how a relatively dense layout makes investment in public transport pay its way. Forty-three per cent of the city's commuters use buses and a light railway system; more than in any other North American city.

Less roads, less car travel

Throughout the industrial world demand for more road space has tended to be matched with ever-

Getting on your bike

There are twice as many bikes in the world as cars – about 800 million in total. In many developing-world cities bicycles and rickshaws are the commonest form of transport. However, in car-dominated cities riding a bike can be precarious: cars and their fumes threaten health and lives. Forward-looking urban authorities have provided bike lanes to improve traffic flow and make cycling safer. Cities built on flat land such as Amsterdam and Oxford have always had thriving populations of bike riders. In the Netherlands, where one-third of all journeys are by bike, Denmark, Japan, and Germany there are bike-and-ride facilities that enable people to take their bikes on public transport and this has proved enormously popular. In the UK three-quarters of all commuting journeys are 8km or less in distance and therefore quite suitable for cycling.

"Cars use 1860 calories per passenger mile, buses 920, rail 885, walking 100, and bicycles only 35 calories per passenger mile."

Professor V. Setty Pendakur, Columbia University

The uphill struggle
The urban cyclist is a symbol of the fight to change attitudes to transportation in cities: risking life and limb the cyclist makes a statement. The bicycle is a cheap, fast, and ecologically friendly way of getting around the city. The more that people insist on using them, the more urban authorities will have to accommodate them.

increasing road construction. But the more roads are built the more they will fill up with cars: traffic will always increase as long as it is cheaper and easier for people to use private vehicles. In California there are roads everywhere yet gridlock is a frequent reality in a state where 90 per cent of journeys are done by private car. In Los Angeles two-thirds of the land area is devoted to roads and parking. If we insist on owning cars, we should do our utmost to change our lives to reduce their routine use. Asserting the right to reasonably priced public transport is vital in an age that has made the motor car a part of our very identity. Good parking facilities at major bus and rail stations, and improved conditions for cyclists are also important measures for reducing our car dependence.

The shape of things to come

Los Angeles, with the highest level of car ownership in the world, has initiated stringent measures to restrict the use of cars, reduce air pollution, and improve mass transit systems. By 2000 40 per cent of all passenger vehicles and 70 per cent of freight vehicles will be required to use "low emission" technologies such as methanol- and electric-powered vehicles. With the ever-growing number of solar- and wind-power stations in California, electricity available for vehicles will come from increasingly clean sources. Emissions of air pollutants such as nitrogen oxides, hydrocarbons, sulphur dioxide, and carbon monoxide are required to be cut by half by 2010, and therefore the automobile industry has a powerful incentive to produce innovative technology that will set new standards worldwide. Hydrogen- and solar-powered vehicles are likely to have largely taken over from petrol-powered ones early in the twenty-first century.

San Francisco light railway

After the 1989 earthquake, when the Bay Area's transportation system suffered severe disruption, the Bay Area Rapid Transport system (BART) enjoyed a tremendous boost. Even after freeways were reopened, BART ridership continued to be up by 25,000 a day from pre-quake levels. Environ-

Traffic calming

Many car-congested inner city areas have found traffic calming to be an effective means of easing the problem. In the Netherlands the "woonerven" system has returned many streets to their former role as social centres. Ramps, humps, street-narrowing, tree-planting, bottlenecks, and bends all contribute to slowing down and discouraging traffic. The aim is to reduce traffic to walking speed, making it possible for streets to be crossed safely and to be used as play areas again. It has been found that such measures greatly increase the social interaction across streets, and bring back a sense of community. The success of Dutch and German experiments with traffic calming has encouraged the adaptation of such concepts in cities throughout the world.

"Wide roads and streams of motor vehicles destroy the function of the street as a locus for social interaction and break community ties. ... The residential street used to be the traditional play space and social milieu for children and provided an introduction for them to a world beyond their family, without their needing to be accompanied to reach it."

Mayer Hillman, *Reviving The City*

Before calming
Streets dedicated to car
travel cause noise and air
pollution, and contribute
to a sense of isolation;
people feel cut off from
each other by the street's
incessant traffic flow.

After calming
Throughout the world the
value of streets as social
centres is being redis-
covered, particularly in
mixed-use areas, which
have the potential for
social life.

mental groups are campaigning to prevent the construction of further freeways by pressurizing for extensions of the public rail system.

Curitiba: the surface metro

The Brazilian city of Curitiba has taken the lead in organizing a particularly rational public transport system. A city of about 1.6 million people has a unique "surface metro", a highly efficient network of fast-running buses, obviating the need for an underground system. The city has built high-speed bus lanes that prevent buses being held up by car traffic. With a bus stop every 400 metres people have convenient access to buses and cylindrical loading tubes allow passengers to pay their fares in advance to speed up the boarding process. One million three hundred thousand passengers use the city's public transport system daily; it is faster and often cheaper than that of other Brazilian cities. The city also has an extensive system of cycle lanes, and traffic calming in selected streets. Despite high car ownership of one car for every five people, car use is lower than in most other Brazilian cities.

New York has taken a close look at Curitiba's surface metro system and hopes to make its own existing bus routes more efficient. A high-speed bus network could serve to improve the linkages between the various transportation systems currently in use in the New York metropolitan region.

Solar cars

Switzerland was the first country to take action in encouraging the development of cars powered by the sun. Since the mid-1980s the country has been organizing grand prize races for solar-powered cars, an incentive that has greatly stimulated technical development. New light-weight car design, new solar cells, new electric motors, and new battery systems have increased the speed and range of solar cars. There are sleek, prototype racing cars as well as production models suitable for urban traffic and commuting. The latter can be plugged into solar panels at home to recharge the batteries. At present these cars are still expensive, but with growing demand will become more affordable.

Amsterdam: car-free plan

In March 1992 the people of Amsterdam voted in their first-ever referendum to ban the 35,000 cars that come into the centre each day. While the referendum was not binding, there is no doubt that this expression of popular opinion will influence the city's transport policy. By throwing out the car Amsterdam would follow Strasbourg, which has banned cars from its centre. The pol-

icy now even has the support of local businesses, whose fear of losing customers proved to be unjustified.

Trams in Amsterdam
Trams (below) and light railways are a realistic short haul transport option, leaving safe space for bicycles and pedestrians.

"Our future is framed by the need to reduce gasoline use, clean up smog, produce less greenhouse gases and stop urban sprawl. Only transit *can adequately cope with these problems . . ."*

Professor Peter Newman, Murdoch University, Australia

From disposal to recycling

For decades waste disposal was cheap and easy. But today, the problems are numerous: too little space left for dumping; increased transport costs; the use of non-biodegradable materials, which remain as persistent trash; co-disposal; and poisons leaching into groundwater (see pp. 98-9). Disposal costs have shot up and now that the environmental cost of waste disposal is brought into economic equations, urban recycling is making progress.

Beyond the throwaway city

Everything in the natural world is recycled; living organisms all eventually die and are converted into new life. This principle needs to be applied to waste material. Recycling of municipal wastes in many cities is still in its infancy. Yet resource-efficiency of cities is crucial for making them sustainable and compatible with the living world. Most wastes can be reused or recycled; making new products from recycled materials not only eases the waste disposal problem it also saves energy and reduces pollution. This principle of recycling can be applied to metals, glass, paper, plastics, organic kitchen wastes, and also sewage (see pp. 162-5). Cities with effective recycling policies have shown that it is possible to recycle three-quarters of the rubbish discarded.

Rich cities, rich pickings

Future generations will have even less access to raw materials and may well be forced to mine urban waste tips for metals, plastics, and glass. The smelly, incongruous mixture of disparate materials would be hard to disentangle. Both waste recycling and waste disposal would be more efficient if "co-disposal" of waste materials was avoided. Some cities, such as Ontario and Sheffield, separate materials before they are discarded and a growing number of cities now have separate collection schemes for different materials.

Recycling or reuse?

Reuse is an even better option than recycling. Glass bottles, in particular, can be used again and again. Why melt down old bottles to make new ones,

Total recycling

Our throwaway society, left to its own devices, could end up discarding its own future. Yet it is quite feasible to replace throwaway consumption with "total" recycling, turning a linear process into a circular one.

Plastics recycling
Plastics create a disposal problem because they persist in the environment. Until recently it was almost impossible to recycle plastics, but today heavy-duty containers and water pipes can be made from recycled plastics. In Germany supermarkets are obliged to take back and recycle any packaging that a customer does not want.

Organic waste recycling

One-fifth of municipal waste is organic kitchen and yard waste. Many cities separate this off and use rotating drums to break it down. France has over 100 composting plants producing 800,000 tonnes of compost a year.

Aluminium recycling

Recycling aluminium to make alu cans makes economic sense. It not only reduces the use of bauxite it also reduces energy consumption and pollution of the production process by 95%. Swedish cities recycle 80% of their alu cans.

Paper recycling

Great environmental and economic savings can be made from recycling paper; using recycled material to make paper uses 30 to 40% less energy than processing virgin pulp. Cities in Japan and the Netherlands currently recycle 50% of their paper.

when the originals can be reused? In British cities milk is delivered in glass bottles, which are used about 24 times each. Glass bottles are traditionally easier to reuse or recycle than plastic ones, however in Switzerland and Brazil plastic bottles are now produced for reuse. In Germany plastic bottles carry a returnable deposit and the manufacturers are obliged to recycle all bottles returned. Denmark has banned the use of "one-way" plastic bottles. More widespread adoption of such practices is vital.

Practical policies: the "Berlin model"

Cities could in theory minimise the importation of raw materials from outside by reusing waste. To achieve this requires effective recycling strategies backed by legislation and incentives. The city of Berlin has developed a feasible model for urban recycling. By offering to supply households with different-coloured and -labelled dustbins for different forms of waste, and by reducing the collection charges for participating households by 50 per cent, the scheme has attracted a large number of participants. Together with the city's recycling banks for glass, paper, and plastics, and dozens of well-advertised recycling yards all over the city, recycling and organic waste composting in Berlin has made rapid progress.

Pollution prevention pays

Individual firms can also develop recycling policies. The North American multinational 3M has practised a policy of pollution prevention and recycling for many years. By product-reformulation, process-modification, equipment-redesign, and recovery and reuse of byproducts, 3M reduced waste and pollution generated by its factories by 50 per cent. It also saved money in the process, no less than $482 million over a decade. The company is now moving toward a policy of zero pollution. Such waste reduction policies of individual companies are a huge help in stemming the deluge of waste from cities. The 3M model is being taken seriously by an ever-growing number of companies for two main reasons: such measures can reduce production costs as well as disposal costs.

Recycling in poor cities

All developing-world megacities have effective recycling systems, with poor people eking out a dangerous living on rubbish dumps. Mountains of mixed garbage are separated into distinct piles of paper, plastic, glass, metal, and bone. These materials are then sold to workshops and factories and used to make new products. In cities such as Cairo, New Mexico, Calcutta, and Lima tens of thousands of people make a living out of recycling trash. For poor cities it is a very cost-effective system, avoiding the need to use large, imported trucks. In Cairo alone over 500 small factories recycle plastics, preventing their disposal and avoiding the unnecessary use of new raw materials.

Phnom Penh, Cambodia
A woman (right) separates the aluminium can tops from their tin bodies prior to selling them to be melted down. Cans are collected from hotels, streets, and rubbish dumps, usually by children.

CHAPTER 7
The responsible city

Cities on a learning curve

To make the functioning of cities compatible with the requirements of an intact biosphere is a tall order. But worldwide, efforts are being made to move in this direction. The learning process involves cities exchanging information with each other on how to tackle the problems they share (see pp. 158-9): developed- and developing-world cities often have more in common with each other than with their own rural hinterlands. Cities have to become more aware of the potential of utilizing the resources on their own doorsteps, and to do so responsibly. Cities need to protect the farmland, forest, and watersheds in their vicinity (see pp. 160-1). That means giving resources back to the land; to create a circular metabolism that ensures a sustainable local food supply (see pp. 162-5).

Global urban responsibility

Today cities have a global hinterland from which they draw their resources and which they affect by their release of greenhouse gases and other wastes. That global impact needs to be matched by a new global sense of urban responsibility (see pp. 166-7). With this in mind some cities in Europe have started "twinning" with other cities and with rural areas in far-flung places. Cities, and their people, need to develop a clearer understanding of the implications of their consumption and discharge patterns. That growing awareness is also leading to greater efforts to reduce the global impact of our cities (see pp. 168-9).

The need for enabling policies

How can cities get off the back of the rest of the world? Part of the answer lies in the shape and density of settlements, though it would be wrong to assume that planning policies will provide all the solutions. Cities have their own dynamics of growth and sustenance. To understand these better is the basis of correct decision-making and appropriate planning. Worldwide enabling policies are needed to provide people with secure, pleasant, and sustainable inner-city habitats, weakening the dynamics of suburban sprawl (see pp. 170-5).

A world of eco-cities

For cities to become sustainable, they need to develop a strong awareness of the ways they affect the world. They must create their own control systems, acting like thermostats, continually monitoring their global and local environmental impacts. Responding to this feedback, eco-cities would take all the necessary measures for global and local ecological rebuilding into their grasp. They would reorganize their transport, energy, food, and sewage systems for maximum efficiency and minimal environmental impact. Eco-cities would acknowledge the limits of the Earth's carrying capacity by nourishing the wellbeing of their local hinterland. Global dependence would be replaced by more sustainable local living.

Negative feedback

Feedback systems
The impact of cities on the environment could be monitored by control
systems detecting conditions to be
regulated. They would register any
variation in a set level, amplify it,
and control inputs to the (urban) system. The amplified variation would
trigger a feedback control: either
positive feedback (bottom left) or
negative feedback (top left), which
would reverse the change.

Cities compete
By establishing set criteria
for urban sustainability,
cities could compete for
"best" environmental per-
formance. The most
resource-efficient cities
could achieve the best
economic performance.

Positive feedback

Urban problem-solving

The exploding cities in the developing world are in a state of "permanent change". Cities such as São Paulo have been growing at the rate of up to 400,000 new inhabitants a year.

As cities evolve so does their need for infrastructure and suitable organizational methods. The decision-making process itself has to be arranged to deal with ever-changing requirements.

The use of innovative concepts is essential and to ensure efficiency of planning the active involvement of local communities in decision-making is essential: people know what they need, and their active role in planning makes a real difference.

Cities teaching each other

Cities can learn from each other's experiences and "twinning" has long been an effective method for bringing the citizens of different cities together. The scheme has also been used for sharing information about improving methods of organization, such as public transport, waste disposal, and planning policy. Large cities the world over have similar problems and systems of information exchange have now been established between them.

The Mega-cities Project

One of the most innovative approaches to urban problem-solving comes from the Mega-cities Project, run since 1987 by Dr Janice Perlman of New York University. She started with the premise that the megacities of the world with over 10 million people have more in common with each other than with the smaller towns and villages in their own countries. According to Dr Perlman "every first-world city has within it a third-world city of malnutrition, infant mortality, homelessness, and unemployment. And conversely, every third-world city has within it a first-world city of high tech, high fashion, and high finance."

Information transfer

Teams from the world's largest cities meet twice a year to discuss effective ways of transferring innovations from one city to another. All projects collated are disseminated for potential adoption by other cities. It is not only the projects themselves that are transferred from city to city but also the institutional methods to implement them. The issues

Citizen's checkpoints

In Calcutta a citizens' action group called "Concern for Calcutta" runs conservation campaigns aimed at improving the city's quality of life. It has set up kiosks to enable neighbourhood residents to access and influence government authorities on environmental issues of their concern. The kiosks are run by staff of the Calcutta Municipal Corporation.

"We are the first generation to live with the problems of the metropolis, or megalopolis. Nobody is really used to organizing space for 15 or 20 million inhabitants in one city, growing by two or three hundred thousand every year, and simultaneously coping with huge social and economic differences. These are new problems, because they are so much larger and we are all learning."

Professor Ladislau Dowbor, São Paulo

range from environmental regeneration, poverty alleviation and income generation, to decentralization and democratization, and women's empowerment. In 1992 the cities involved in the Mega-cities project included Bangkok, Beijing, Bombay, Buenos Aires, Curitiba, Delhi, Jakarta, London, Los Angeles, Mexico City, Moscow, New York, Rio de Janeiro, Sâo Paulo, and Tokyo.

Disseminating know-how

The Mega-cities Project acts as an information conduit between governments, city authorities, business and community leaders. Its purpose is to shorten the time-lag between the emergence of innovative ideas and their implementation and diffusion. All too often cities are not even aware of worthwhile projects that are occurring, often initiated by disadvantaged communities themselves.

The urban poor suffer disproportionately from makeshift services and environmental degradation. But these very problems are also a spur for social innovation. The Mega-cities Project has disseminated solutions to the problems of poor communities ranging from food distribution, waste recycling, water conservation and sanitation, self-help building, tree planting, ecological restoration of wasteland, to gardens for disabled people. In most cases the needs of local communities are partly met by their own efforts and partly by help from support groups and urban authorities.

Mega-cities Project: practical problem-solving

The following examples of Mega-city initiatives show how much the developing world can teach the developed world:

✳ Sâo Paulo publicly displays air pollution monitors and restricts car traffic in the city centre when pollution is too high. New York is adapting this system for its own purposes.

✳ In Delhi mobile crèches provide on-site education and daycare for children of migrant construction workers. This is being adopted by Mexico City. Delhi's system of night shelters for the homeless is being adopted by New York.

✳ In Bangkok children are being educated by imaginative TV programmes, cartoons, posters, and school campaigns to stop littering and to keep streets tidy. Los Angeles, London, Tokyo, and Rio are now developing similar campaigns.

"There is enough energy and creativity in the cities today to address the problems, but too few mechanisms to channel these forces into the policy-making process, or to multiply the effects of approaches that work. The seeds of tomorrow's solutions can be found in today's experiences, but need to be carefully sought out within each sector, neighbourhood, and policy area. We know too much about failures and needs, too little about the successes. . . . Circular, rather than linear, systems for water, garbage, sewerage, energy, and food, will have significant implications not only for the cities and their hinterlands but also for sustainable development worldwide."

"We urgently need to find new approaches which better utilize our abundant human resources, our precious natural resources, and our scarce financial resources."

Janice Perlman, Mega-Cities Project

Utilizing the land

Today the quest is on for settlements to establish sustainable relationships with the surrounding countryside. Modern cities would do well to understand how farming communities in former times utilized the land that provided them with their sustenance.

The isolated state

The German geographer Von Thünen showed how self-sufficient settlements in an "isolated state" have a relationship of mutual dependence with the land that surrounds them. He illustrated this relationship as a system of concentric circles (see diagram right). Von Thünen's views have been confirmed by studies of isolated communities in many parts of the world, though there are local variations. Such land-use systems fall into disuse as transport systems and access to distant markets reduce dependence on produce from nearby farms and forests. Increasingly food and timber is being traded on a global basis (see pp. 88-9 and 92-3).

Cities and bioregions

But today the folly of ignoring local sources of food supply is becoming more apparent. Ironically it is in North America, whose cities are least reliant on their own food production, that such ideas are being revived. The concept of "bioregionalism" has grown out of the realization that long-distance food trade could disappear as cheap fossil fuels, and transport systems that rely on them, become a thing of the past.

Nurturing the hinterland

Bioregionalism is not solely concerned with the food supply for cities from their hinterlands. Bioregionalists argue that cities have grown away from dependence on the surrounding landscape, as small farming settlements expand into trading and industrial centres. But today cities need to nurture their relationship with their hinterlands, ensuring a local food supply, and water supplies from sustainable nearby sources. This implies protecting watersheds from which they tap their supplies.

Safeguarding city hinterlands

Cities need to ensure the continuity of local ecosystems that existed before they did: places of great natural diversity such as forested mountains, hillsides, meadows, creeks, and lakes. Their health and integrity ensures the continuity of all local life, including the human population.

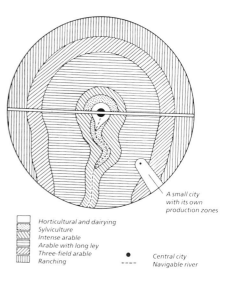

A small city with its own production zones

Horticultural and dairying	
Sylviculture	
Intense arable	
Arable with long ley	
Three-field arable	● Central city
Ranching	- - - - Navigable river

Von Thünen's land use system
Close to the settlement (diagram above) is a ring of vegetable gardens. Outside this are grazing orchards producing fruit and poultry. Beyond are forests for firewood and building timber, while further out are fields for growing grain and vegetables.

Wandiphodrang village, Bhutan
The settlement (right) has a rich bioregion comprising a lake, woods, agricultural terraces, wooded foothills, and a mountain watershed beyond.

Fertility exchange

Every day hundreds of thousands of tonnes of food are transported from rural areas to the world's cities. With these crops, plant nutrients such as nitrogen, potash, and phosphates are removed from the land for ever, ending up as urban sewage. To make cities sustainable it is critical for the fertility contained in that sewage to be returned to the land. Some towns and cities in history (see pp. 44-5) have kept their farmlands productive by recycling human wastes, but most have undermined their potential fertility by discarding them (see pp. 40-1).

Asian cities and their fertile land

Most countries in Asia have long practised a system of "nightsoil recycling", which helps to ensure the ecological viability of their cities by using human waste to compost agricultural land. Formerly this was done using buckets and handcarts, but today special vacuum tankers are used if possible. Pipelines for transporting urban sewage back to farming areas could also be envisaged.

Urban growth and sewage recycling

China's cities have grown more slowly than cities in other parts of the world, despite the country's very rapid population growth. In 1981 only 14 per cent of China's population lived in cities – one of the lowest percentages in the world – and 6 per cent lived in the agricultural suburbs. Keeping urban populations low was achieved by deliberate rural development policies, which, particularly in recent years, have greatly improved rural living conditions. The slow growth of cities made it possible to maintain the food production of the outer suburbs, based on composted human wastes, without the land being built over by new housing developments. Many rapidly expanding developing-world cities would find it more difficult to maintain land on the urban fringe for the purposes of food production. However, the stabilized large cities of Europe and North America might, once again, adopt policies of fertility exchange between cities and their surrounding countryside, using modern sewage recycling technologies.

China's eco-cities

Of China's 15 largest cities, 14 have their own farm belts and, until recently, were largely self-sufficient in food. Even today, substantial quantities of the food required by major cities such as Beijing, Shanghai, Tianjin, Shenyang, Wuhan, and Guangzhou come from their own agricultural suburbs, from land on which human waste is used as fertilizer. The rural adjunct to these cities, or xian, supplies vegetables, grain, fruit, and meat required by the city's inhabitants. However, rapid industrialization of China's cities, and the associated wealth, is now causing these sustainable urban land-use systems to come under question. Road building and house construction is now covering some former urban-fringe farmland. It remains to be seen whether China's cities will still be "eco-cities" in 20 years' time.

Traditional Chinese city farming cycle
The farm belt (right) keeps the city supplied with all the food it needs: in return the city gives back its human and organic kitchen waste to sustain the soil.

The kidneys of the urban organism

In Australia a revolutionary new sewage processing system has been developed by Memtec, a company that first made a name marketing kidney machines. Their compact sewage plants are a logical development of the membrane technology developed for artificial kidneys.

The Memtec system

Memtec's processors filter waste water released by cities: the machines are capable of intercepting 97 to 99 per cent of all contaminants, including human wastes, bacteria, viruses, heavy metals, and oil. The treatment takes a fraction of the time required by conventional sewage plants – the system is capable of removing solid particles in five minutes rather than five hours. Therefore bioreactors can be far more compact and installed separately in residential and industrial areas, avoiding contamination of household sewage with industrial effluents. Old fashioned waste treatment systems require one million litres of water to transport only 200 litres of waste, but with the Memtec system water for carrying the wastes is dramatically reduced and there is no need for chlorine. The resulting water is almost pure and can be recycled into drinking water.

Cost-effective treatment

The overall cost of the process is about the same as conventional systems: the actual technology is more expensive, but because water use is greatly reduced the cost is less. Since the bioreactors require only one-sixth of the space needed for conventional sewage works, land cost is far lower. Memtec envisage installing compact neighbourhood sewage systems throughout cities, greatly reducing the need for massive underground pipes. Their systems are in operation in several cities in Japan, Britain, North America, and Australia. Sydney has four such plants so far. Memtec says that if its plants were installed throughout the city the water contamination off famous Bondi Beach, the "sewer of the South Pacific", would be a thing of the past, and the sewage could be used to fertilize farmland.

Renovating waste water

Penn State University in North America has experimented with an innovative disposal technique for over 30 years. Water from a sewage-treatment facility for 70,000 people is pumped into a forest covering 200 hectares. The nutrients stimulate tree growth; white spruce trees have diameters more than double those of "untreated" forests and the earthworm population is eight times that of "ordinary" forests. Studies over 20 years by Dr William Sopper revealed that the groundwater below the forest used to absorb the sewage continued to be of drinking quality.

The living filter concept
*Waste water works with
the natural system (below)
to irrigate forests and
agricultural land.*

The process
*1 Infiltration to reservoir
2 Precipitation 3 Evap-
oration and transpira-
tion 4 Sewage plant 5
Effluent 6 Well field 7 Bio-
logic complex 8 Ground
water reservoir 9 Dis-
charge to springs and
wells 10 Ground water
recharge 11 Renovation
zone 12 Water table*

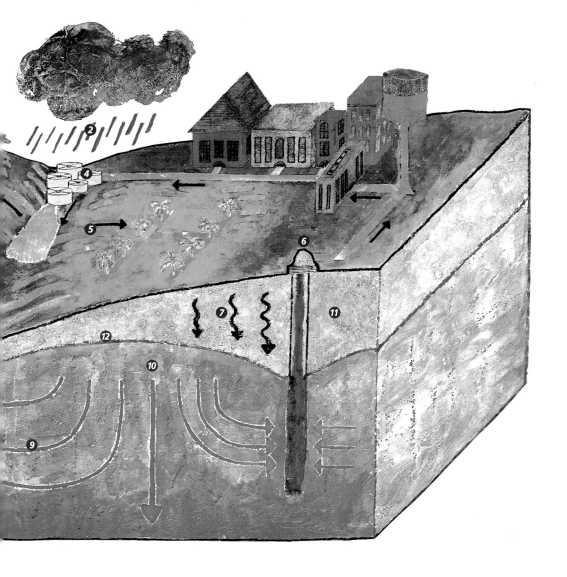

A desert planet?

The appetite of cities for the world's resources, and their discharge of solid, liquid and gaseous wastes, is in danger of turning the planet into a desert. Yet the biocidic role of cities (see pp. 22-3) could be reversed by growing environmental awareness and a new sense of global responsibility. Improving the efficiency of the functioning of cities can vastly reduce their impact on the planet. Enormous improvements in their performance can be achieved by redesigning city metabolism and giving priority to circular processes. However, even then cities will continue burning fossil fuels (see pp. 106-7) and will therefore continue to release greenhouse gases (see pp. 112-13) – a fundamental problem that must be addressed urgently.

Global commitment

Cities use between two-thirds and three-quarters of the global consumption of fossil fuels. Even if this was significantly reduced it would continue to contribute to the build-up of carbon dioxide (CO_2) in the atmosphere. One of the few things we can do about this is not further reduce the world's vegetation cover, as we have done for centuries, but actually increase it instead. Only by provision of large areas of vegetation can the waste gases released by cities be·absorbed through photosynthesis. Plants, and particularly trees, store carbon from the atmosphere as they grow. Cities need to nurture forests as "symbiotic partners" to ensure climatic stability. But achieving this means making commitments on a global scale.

Protection of tropical forests is one expression of concern about our impact on the biosphere. Cities are the major consumers of the world's tropical timber, but now many of them are turning from poachers into gamekeepers. In 1992 over 400 town and city councils in continental Europe had committed themselves to boycotts of tropical hardwoods, informing householders, architects, and builders about the problems of tropical deforestation and about more sustainable alternatives to the use of tropical hardwoods.

Climate protection

Cities by definition are built-up areas, where the human species dominates the natural world. Urban forestry can help to absorb urban waste gases to a

The European Climate Alliance
The Alliance, which includes cities such as Munich, Nuremberg, Berlin, Frankfurt, Vienna, Salzburg, Arnhem, Utrecht, Schiedam, and Geneva concerns itself with three main tasks:
● The target of reducing urban CO_2 emissions by half by 2010. Meetings are held on how to improve the energy efficiency of households and traffic systems.
● Safeguarding rainforest areas of South America by linking up with indigenous and traditional communities in Peru and Brazil. The idea is to "twin" cities in Europe with forest tribes and rural communities in the Amazon, meeting regularly with representatives.
● Giving financial support to indigenous communities to help them protect their forests and set up sustainable farming systems based on traditional techniques.

Declaration of the Climate Alliance

"We European cities support the interest of the Indian people of the Amazon in safeguarding the tropical rainforests, the basis of their existence, through land titles and the sustainable use of Indian territories. By defending the forests and rivers they contribute to the integrity of the Earth's atmosphere as a basic condition for assuring future human life. ... In the effort to preserve adequate conditions of life on Earth we see ourselves as their partners in an alliance to preserve tropical forests and world climate."

limited extent. But the CO_2 released by cities permeates the atmosphere worldwide. Cities have started to respond to this reality by acting on a global basis. In Canada the International Council on Local Environmental Initiatives (ICLEI) (see pp. 36-7) has started to spread awareness about the release of CO_2 and other greenhouse gases by cities. In Europe this realization has led over one hundred cities to come together in an organization called the Climate Alliance (see right). In 1990 the environment department of the city of Frankfurt initiated the foundation of the Alliance in realization that cities have the capacity to act locally to reduce CO_2 emissions, to improve the energy efficiency of cities, and globally to help safeguard the integrity of forest ecosystems. Until the 1990s, international concern over tropical rainforests overshadowed the considerable problems of Canada and, less accessibly, Siberia, where "clearcutting" (logging) of vast areas of "old growth" forests is widespread.

Reforestation projects

A further step will be for cities to actually initiate re-vegetation or re-forestation projects worldwide. There are vast areas in Africa, Australia, Asia, and South America that are denuded of trees and turning into wasteland. Such areas are suitable for conversion to agroforestry systems in which people could be permanently settled, on a sustainable basis, cultivating a great variety of fruit and nut trees and other food crops.

Such attempts at community-based reforestation could be supported by cities keen to help restore the planet's tree cover for the sake of countering global warming and the spread of wasteland, as well as human destitution. There are several agroforestry villages which have been established on former wasteland in the Brazilian and Peruvian Amazon, proving that such land can be revived and made to yield again.

It has been estimated that reforestation, with growing trees, of four million square kilometres worldwide would absorb the four billion tonnes of CO_2 which are added annually to the planet's atmosphere. Initiatives for community-based reforestation involving sustainable agroforestry systems and not vast plantations of identical eucalyptus or pine trees are being considered by support groups in European and North American cities.

Future resources in the balance

The carefree lifestyle of a young urban person today could help to deplete the very resources needed in old age. But the gradual awareness of limits to consumption is reorientating both our lifestyles and our planning concepts. Taking account of the needs of future generations means making decisions today to redevelop our cities into sustainable systems, but as yet the right to an adequate resource supply has not been enshrined in law.

Infinite expectations

Many cities take resources for granted, somehow expecting infinite supplies of finite resources. Currently future availability is determined solely by the price of goods on the market. But is this an adequate concept for regulating the supplies required by cities? We would do well to estimate the interests of future urban generations.

Resource profligacy

Phosphates are forecast to run out within decades and there are no substitutes. Crops cannot grow without them, yet few cities recapture more than a small proportion of phosphates from sewage and current profligacy is endangering the chances of future generations. Today an urbanized humanity is using some 40 per cent of the planet's photosynthetic capacity, and this figure is still rising. Soon there will be little land left that does not produce crops for human consumption.

Resource efficiency

But it need not be that way. Resource efficiency can reduce the land requirements of cities. For example, citizens of Hong Kong eating traditional Chinese cuisine consisting of vegetables, fish, rice, pork, and duck, require only 0.57 hectares of farmland per person, compared with Sydney, which requires 1.12 hectares per head, consuming salad foods, wheat, milk, mutton, and beef. Cities with a high degree of food self-sufficiency are in existence now, but it will take decades to develop infrastructures for converting "conventional" cities to greater sustainability.

How can we safeguard the interests of future urban generations? It is not good enough to bequeath them urban structures that require unlimited supplies of cheap fuels to function viably. All forecasts suggest that oil will be in short supply within a few decades.

Throughout history cities have raised taxes to control local consumption patterns. Today energy and resources taxes are widely discussed and people such as the British economist Farrell Bradbury have suggested that they could be raised as local taxes.

In the red or the green?
The typical urban lifestyle, with its linear metabolism, puts us in the red on the resource scales for future generations. To make the needle swing the other way we must devise circular metabolisms, using "green" principles.

"Reduced dependence on external supplies of resources will increase the stability, diversity, and resilience of the urban ecosystem."

Ken Newcombe et al,
"The Metabolism of a City: the Case of Hong Kong", Ambio 7, 1978

Upward and outward

Post-war urban development has received much criticism. There is a universal feeling that the convivial city (see pp. 118-19), with its close-knit neighbourhoods, workshops, cafés, shops, markets, and cultural centres has been sacrificed to an anonymous landscape of tower blocks, shopping malls, and suburban sprawl. Cities have surged upward and outward, losing their all-important sense of social cohesion. Suburban homes set in spacious gardens and multi-laned motorways for commuting to jobs in the inner city have swallowed up farmland on the urban fringe. The energy inefficiency of such low-density sprawl is difficult to accept in a world threatened by global warming (see pp. 112-13) and hugely depleted reserves of fossil fuels.

Compact city or rural resettlement?

Today the search is on for suitable designs for compact cities. Throughout the developed world powerful moves are afoot to contain urban sprawl and to bring intimacy back into cities. But Ebenezer Howard's Garden City concept, of creating a spacious city in the garden (see pp. 54-5), has not been forgotten. There is a strong, continuing desire to reinstate the countryside in inner cities in the hope of attracting people back to the city centre, *and*, in addition, to allow those who wish to do so to migrate to new purpose-built garden cities, constructed on green-field sites. Is it possible to reconcile these two, seemingly opposite, positions?

Back to the future?

In North America in the 1960s urbanist Jane Jacobs published her seminal book *The Death and Life of Great American Cities*. It stimulated a new interest in dense cities with vigorous street lives. In recent years the European Community (EC) has issued directives to revive the concept of compact cities, last seen in medieval Europe (see pp. 44-5). Cities that have survived from medieval days such as Verona, Urbino, and Freiburg, with their bustling centres, particularly impressed the planners. Efforts are also being made to renovate and revive inner-city areas and substantial financial support is now

Davis, California

The city of Davis, near Sacramento, harbours a remarkable experiment in urban living. Village Homes, consisting of some 200 houses, designed by Peter Calthorpe and Michael Corbett, is a community of people who all share the goal of urban sustainability. It is an experiment in "urban permaculture", the close integration of houses, orchards, and vegetable gardens. The city as a whole has

some of the most advanced recycling systems anywhere in California: 70% of the population
voluntarily sort their rubbish for
recycling. Davis has imposed its own
limits to growth by a process of
democratic planning: the intention
is to stop growing at 50,000 people.

Village Homes, Davis
*Despite the hot climate,
residents (below) largely
manage without air-con-
ditioners. Some 20,000
trees shade the houses,
making Davis look like a
city in a forest.*

available to make central zones car-free and pedestrianized. The removal of cars from centres revitalizes pedestrian street life, with shops, markets, and cafés drawing in the people.

Proximity revisited

The EC's position closely matches that of countryside protection groups throughout Europe and North America who are trying to prevent the further encroachment of rural areas by urban growth. They too see the need to revive inner cities and to utilize any existing wasteland as a way of halting urban sprawl. The concept of "proximity", urban layout and zoning, which allows people to live, work, and shop without travelling great distances, is rapidly gaining new currency. Unfortunately compact urban development could mean a shortage of space for parks, gardens, and allotments, robbing urban citizens of vital encounters with nature.

Reinhabiting the land

Urbanization in developed countries is typically between 70 and 80 per cent. Should there not be a more equal balance between town and country? Many people think so, and the dream of de-urbanization, of people moving to the country to live close to nature, has never completely died. Since the 1960s millions of people in the developed world have voted with their feet and moved to rural areas, while others dream of *reinhabiting* the land and of living in "new" rural villages with energy-efficient homes surrounded by gardens and orchards. But all over Europe and in some parts of North America, such projects have been rejected by planning authorities for the sake of protecting the countryside and only a handful of these new ideas has actually been realized. Yet growing minorities aspire to a self-reliant rural lifestyle, particularly since modern communications technology can help people exchange commuting for *tele*-commuting.

The age of the "office-anywhere"

The choices offered by the "micro-revolution" are greatly influencing living patterns, in both city and country. It is now a reality, not just a dream, to be able to set up an "electronic home", since many kinds of work can now be done independently at home, without the need to travel daily to an office. Equipped with word processor, fax machine, and

Permaculture

This philosophy of farming and gardening, first devised by Bill Mollison in Australia, aims for sustainable self-sufficiency on an area of land. It harmonizes organic food-growing with livestock rearing and forestry, incorporating a far greater diversity of crops than is usual.

Lightmoor Village, Telford

In Britain the Town and Country Planning Association initiated the Lightmoor Village development on the outskirts of Telford with the support of that city's development corporation. The Village has shown that it is possible for people to build their own small settlement, allowing for a flexible lifestyle combining part-time employment or self-employment with organic vegetable growing. At the presentation at which the scheme won top prize, Prince Charles spoke of the "spaghetti bolognese of red tape" that prevents the man in the street from influencing his own surroundings: a comment that profoundly influenced attitudes to forward-thinking planning.

Co-housing schemes

Co-housing, or co-operative housing, is a new concept both for "infill development" within cities and for green-field sites. Originating in Denmark, co-housing is now flourishing in North America, too. Building sites capable of accommodating between 15 and 35 houses are suitable for this type of development. The idea is simple, yet revolutionary, reviving the old-established concept of the urban neighbourhood, with its many varied amenities. Each household group has its own residence, but there are also community facilities such as shared dining halls, children's playrooms, workshops, guest rooms, and laundries. According to Charles Durrett and Kathryn McCamant residents participate in the planning of their shared development and the layout is designed specifically to encourage participation. Residents manage their own community, co-operating with each other to meet continually changing needs.

modern people can alternate work for money with work in the vegetable garden. Some "rural resettlers" have even decided that the time spent earning money to buy food may as well be spent actually growing some of it.

The case for new villages

Advocates for rural resettlement say: Why not allow changes in planning laws to allow for "community development licences" in rural areas? The development of ecologically sensitive, sustainable communities in rural areas could be a realistic alternative to suburban sprawl. This could, for example, occur on existing farms when they come up for sale. Small areas of land on such farms could be developed into new, compact hamlets or villages, therefore avoiding further unnecessary encroachment of productive land. Some arable land could be converted into vegetable plots and orchards possibly making use of the practice of permaculture (see p. 172). Much of the land, however, could be farmed commercially by a farmer employed by the villagers, who in turn would probably earn their living with other pursuits, some could telecommute, while others could convert farm buildings into workshops or small industrial units.

Fighting urban dereliction

However, most planners do not agree with such ideas. They go against the grain of existing planning policies in industrialized countries, which assume that the land must be protected from the people. Planners today tend to advocate that priority should be given to building housing on urban wasteland. In Britain alone 70,000 hectares, or 5 per cent, of urban land is lying derelict as a result of old industries being closed down. A similar situation prevails in parts of Europe and North America, and there are large areas of undeveloped land in many developing-world cities.

The country re-enters the city

People must be given the opportunity to live more closely to nature in this post-industrial era. Rather than cramming inner-city land with houses it should be set aside and used for more mixed development, allowing the country to re-enter the city, creating space for new urban farms, orchards, and neighbourhood gardens. The greening of urban areas today is as much a necessity as the carefully planned "re-inhabitation" of those rural areas that have been deprived of people. City and country are a continuum; their relationship should be encouraged to be mutually beneficial rather than oppositional.

Which way to the future?

Everyone agrees that we must do everything possible to revitalize our cities, but this should mean more than just packing them with people once again. Above all today we need settlements that have a solid basis of employment, where the citizens have the opportunity to get to know one another and where they have the chance to shape community life. People must be able to *re-inhabit* both city and countryside, but they must be allowed to do so in economically, ecologically, and socially sustainable ways. It is apparent now that high-density, low-rise urban living has great advantages for social interaction in cities. But people also need green spaces and the option of growing things to experience a sense of self-reliance and benefit from nature. We have come from nature and we must never lose contact with it, even in the inner city. The proximity of home and workplace is a goal we should all be striving for, enabling people to move around on foot or by bicycle. This should also extend to a more rural lifestyle in a post-industrial age, in which fewer people will work in a conventional factory, or office, environment.

Successful cities

Whatever happens most of us will continue to live in cities. It is therefore critical to make them a success in environmental terms. That means redesigning the urban fabric and also the urban metabolism.

"What we term 'sustainability' was a reality inherent in many preindustrial cultures. It was built into their beliefs, their practises, and the design of their environment. . . . Our vision is that what is sacred is our relation to life and living processes . . . can be made manifest in the design of our everyday environment. . . . The continuity of a culture is carried in its architecture, urban design, and planning."

Sim van der Ryn and Peter Calthorpe, *Sustainable Communities*

"We believe the dangers of continuing in our present ways of building to be very grave, and the promise of ecocity building to be nothing less than learning at last how human beings can coexist in harmony with all other life forms on our home planet."

Richard Register, EcoCity Conference 1990

Street art, New York
Even if the green of the countryside cannot always infiltrate the inner city, creative man-made forms can be stimulating and fun.

Cities for children
*Cities must become places for chil-
dren again: where streets are safe
enough to play; where green spaces
let them experience nature; where
it is a pleasure for them to spend
their lives.*

Play in the city
*Police block off a Harlem
street to cars (above) so
that children can play
safely and freely.*

New directions for sustainable urban living

Every week urban growth corresponding to a large city the size of Birmingham, Adelaide, Kitakyushu, or Aleppo occurs on the face of the Earth. Gaia, the living planet, cannot cope with such an unprecedented expansion of cities – unless we can make them function *sustainably*. This requires comprehensive new approaches to urban planning and organization.

At present cities do not have to account for their resource impact, nor for how they affect their local and global hinterlands. Their annual budgets are concerned only with cashflows, incomes, and expenditure. But city dwellers are starting to demand that urban authorities assess their inflow of resources and their outflow of wastes, and question the very nature of their cities' metabolisms. For cities to become sustainable they must develop circular metabolisms.

According to the International Union for the Conservation of Nature, "sustainable development improves people's quality of life within the context of the Earth's carrying capacity". This is one of the most pertinent definitions of the concept of sustainability. The massive urban use of non-renewable resources, such as fuels and ores, evidently exceeds that carrying capacity. But cities also mine resources that should be renewable, such as forests and farmland, with little concern for long-term consequences. In future, cities must function in very different ways, in symbiosis with the Earth's environment, or they will terminally undermine their own survival and that of their inhabitants.

Limits to urban growth
There must be limits to urban growth and city size, but no one yet has the full measure of how large cities should be or could be and still be healthy, non-parasitic places. Urban growth the world over has been occurring at the expense of rural life. By helping to maintain a healthy countryside, cities also prevent their own excessive growth.

Cities need to re-establish a healthy and mutually enriching relationship between town and country. In some instances it will be possible to reverse the flow of people to the cities and to initiate a revival of rural community life.

Building the city
Construction workers in
Mexico City (above).

In an urban context sustainability means a wide range of things, such as:

- Resource budgeting
- Energy conservation and efficiency
- Renewable energy technology
- Long-lasting built structures
- Proximity between home and work
- Efficient public transport systems
- Waste reduction and recycling
- Organic waste composting
- A circular metabolism
- Supply of staple foods from local sources

To achieve such far-reaching goals, citizens (especially planners) need a new model to follow – based on ecological principles and designed to achieve a circular metabolism. Unfortunately such an integrated model does not yet exist, since contemporary cities do not conceptualize their relationship to the rest of the world in this way. But many cities have pioneered elements of this model from which others can learn: Stockholm has high standards of building insulation; Helsinki has one of the most advanced systems of combined heat and power; Californian cities are making rapid progress with solar and wind energy; Canadian cities are developing the healthy cities concept; cities such as Curitiba have highly efficient public transport systems, and São Paulo powers its buses by methane gas derived from waste. A city that had all these ingredients would come close to being fully sustainable.

But putting sustainable urban systems into practice requires more than this new model offers. It demands wholly new organizational approaches. In most cities housing, parks, health, employment, transport, electricity, water, gas, waste disposal, and sewage disposal are all organized by separate departments or companies, with only limited links with one another. This rigid structure is a major barrier to greater urban sustainability. By collaboration, city departments can achieve a more efficient use of resources. Furthermore, *all* departments need an environmental brief – separate departments devoted to "the environment" can become marginalized, dealing only with trivial issues.

Cities are losing their distinct identities. Identification often goes no further than supporting the local football team. Urban life is controlled by outside forces, such as multinational companies with shops and factories in the city but few allegiances to it. These forces dominate the economic life of cities and devalue them as social centres. Swamping commercial developments have damaged employment networks and our restless way of life has become a "mobilization" rather than a "civilization".

Making cities fit for people to enjoy is one of the great tasks ahead. They should allow us to live and work locally: we need multi-centred cities with streets for working and streets for walking. We must also take into account the other forms of life that increasingly inhabit our cities – so that they are a fit home for all species.

Cities and city people can use all available funds to invest in sustainable urban living. The structure of cities is their most lasting legacy and prudent investments can make them more sustainable. Rather than wholesale redevelopment cities need to reuse and renew their built-in inheritance. Cities should be places where we can all feel as some of our ancestors did: that we are making cities to be proud of and where future generations will be proud to take our place.

Culture in the city
An open-air concert (above) to celebrate the destruction of the Berlin Wall and the reunification of East and West Germany in 1990.

Centres of excellence
Cities have always been centres of
human endeavour and artistic
excellence, but this has sometimes
been mislaid, or even completely
lost, in the struggle to keep cities
going. It will be crucial to bring
that function of cities back into
the centre of our lives. We need
spaces in which people can come
together to celebrate the creativity
of urban life.

The world's 40 largest cities

We can make a number of observations from this chart (below and continued on pp. 184-5):

• *27 out of the 40 largest cities are in the developing world; the remaining 13 are in the developed world.*

• *The cities of the developing world will grow much faster between 1990 and the year 2000 than those of the developed world.*

• *The survey of persons per room, percentage of income spent on food, percentage of homes with water and electricity, and telephones owned reflect the standards of living of the well-off as well as the very poor.*

• *The highest murder rate for these 40 cities is in Cairo. Latin American cities associated with crime and drugs (Mexico City,*

	Bangalore	Bangkok	Beijing	Bogotá	Bombay	Buenos Aires	Cairo	Calcutta
Ranking in 1990	35	24	11	36	9	8	16	7
Population in 1990 (millions)	5.0	7.2	10.8	4.8	11.2	11.5	9.0	11.8
Population in 2000 (millions)	8.2	10.3	14.0	6.4	15.4	12.9	11.8	15.7
Persons per room	2.8	3.2	1.2	1.5	4.2	1.3	1.5	3.0
% Income spent on food	62	36	52	22	57	40	47	60
% Homes with water/electricity	67	76	89	89	85	86	94	60
Telephones per 100 people	2	12	2	18	5	14	3	2
Infant deaths per 100,000 live births	48	27	11	19	59	21	53	46
Murders per 100,000 people	2.8	7.6	2.5	21.1	1.1	7.6	56.4	1.1
% Children in secondary school*	60	71	97	80	49†	51	53	49†
Levels of ambient noise (1-10)	4	7	4	4	5	3	7	4
Traffic / km. p.h. in rush hour	25.6	20.8	41.1	19.8	16.6	47.6	19.8	21.3
Clean air (score out of ten)	3	3	1	5	3	7	–	1

* Between ages 14 and 17 † Data estimated § Score estimated based on experts' data. Sources: "World Urbanization Prospects 1990", United Nations, New York, 1991 (population statistics) "Cities: life in the world's 100 largest metropolitan areas", Population Crisis Committee, Washington, 1990

Rio de Janeiro, São Paulo, and Bogotá) have the next highest rates, followed by North American cities.

• Pollution (air and noise) are generally higher in cities of the developing world because of lax anti-pollution laws and inefficient production methods.

• Traffic congestion is similar in very large cities everywhere.

• The number of infant deaths reflects levels of health care and poverty; Karachi and Dhaka are the worst affected.

• The percentage of children in secondary school shows the highly individual nature of education systems worldwide; for instance, London scores lower than Mexico City.

Chicago	Delhi	Dhaka	Hong Kong	Istanbul	Jakarta	Karachi	Lagos	Lahore	Lima	London	Los Angeles
25	18	28	31	27	15	23	22	39	29	13	6
7.0	8.8	6.6	5.4	6.7	9.3	7.7	7.7	4.1	6.2	10.4	11.9
7.3	13.2	12.2	6.1	9.5	13.7	11.7	12.9	5.9	8.2	10.5	13.9
0.5	2.4	3.1	1.6	1.6	3.4	3.3	5.8	4.5	2.3	0.6	0.5
13	40	63	38	60	45	43	58	45	70	14	0.9
97	40	73	97	89	45	75	50	80	82	100	94
53	5	2	42	18	3	2	1	3	2	50	35†
12	40	108	7	59	45	65	85	83	34	10	9
10.6	4.1	2.4	1.5	3.5	5.3	5.7	–	4.8	–	2.5	12.4
93	49	37	86	67	77	97	31	32	55	58	90
5	5	4	5	7	6	9	7	8	7	8	6
34.1	22.4	34.2	19.5	17.9	26.1	28.2	27.8	21.4	5.9	16.6	30.4
6	1	–	8	–	1	9	–	9	–	7	3

The world's 40 largest cities (continued)

The limits of the city. As each country has its own way of delineating cities, there is a worldwide problem in establishing comparative population figures. Chinese cities (see pp. 162-3) control large areas of land around them, where food is grown for urban supplies. The people who live there, however, are not necessarily included in population census figures. According to David Satterthwaite, in the Philippines alone there are eight different ways of defining a city. Each definition reaches a different conclusion on the numbers of people in Manila.

How big are the world's largest cities? The world's largest cities are far larger than any previous human settlements. In 1990 12 cities had populations over 10 million people and 4 had over 15 million people (see pp. 64-5 and 70-1). Some of the largest cities are experiencing a continuing population influx and natural increases in existing popula-

	Madras	Madrid	Manila	Mexico City	Milan	Moscow	New York	Osaka
Ranking in 1990	30	33	19	2	32	17	4	20
Population in 1990 (millions)	5.7	5.2	8.5	20.2	5.3	8.8	16.2	8.5
Population in 2000 (millions)	7.8	5.9	11.8	25.6	5.4	9.0	16.8	8.6
Persons per room	2.9	0.5	3.0	1.9	0.8	1.3	0.5	0.6
% Income spent on food	33	26	38	41	21	33	16	18
% Homes with water/electricity	76	100	91	94	99	100	99	98
Telephones per 100 people	2	38	9	6	75	39	56	42
Infant deaths per 100,000 live births	44	10	36	36	8	20	10	5
Murders per 100,000 people	1.1	0.6	30.5	27.6	2.5	7.0	12.8	1.7
% Children in secondary school*	56	88	67	62	75	100	95	97
Levels of ambient noise (1-10)	8	8	4	6	6	6	8	4
Traffic / km. p.h. in rush hour	20.8	23.8	11.5	12.8	26.6	50.4	13.9	35.8
Clean air (score out of ten)	–	5	6	2	1	3	5	9

* Between ages 14 and 17 † Data estimated § Score estimated based on experts' data. Sources: "World Urbanization Prospects 1990", United Nations, New York, 1991 (population statistics) "Cities: life in the world's 100 largest metropolitan areas", Population Crisis Committee, Washington, 1990

tions that are very hard to monitor or to control. Population censuses in cities such as São Paulo, Cairo, Lagos, Bombay, or Bangkok are out of date as soon as they have been completed. This contrasts with "mature" cities such as London whose population has been virtually static for decades.

Financial and industrial world capital? The world's largest city is not Mexico City, as has often been claimed, but Tokyo-Yokohama. These two cities have grown together into one vast megalopolis, now the world's largest and most powerful industrial and financial centre. No other city demonstrates as clearly the industrial and financial base of urban growth, due to the astonishing industrial success of Japan. Tokyo-Yokohama is the greatest manifestation of the shift in economic prowess away from Europe and America to Asia.

Paris	Philadelphia	Rio de Janeiro	St. Petersburg	Santiago	São Paulo	Seoul	Shanghai	Shenyang	Tehran	Tianjin	Tokyo-Yokohama
21	40	12	34	38	3	10	5	37	26	14	1
8.5	4.3	10.7	5.1	4.7	17.4	11.0	13.4	4.8	6.8	9.4	23.4
8.6	4.5	12.5	5.4	5.6	22.1	12.7	17.0	6.3	8.5	12.7	24.2
0.8†	0.4	0.8	1.5	1.3	0.8	2.0	2.0	2.5	1.3	1.2	0.9
21	14	26	32	42	50	34	55	52	–	52	18
99	100	92	100	91	100	100	95	66	84	82	100
44	56	8	31	9	16	22	4	3	–	4	44
12	13	40	19	16	37	12	14	13	54	15	5
2.4	11.5	36.6	7.3	7.4	26.0	1.2	2.5	2.3	–	2.5	1.4
99	95	55	93	86	67	90	94	83	58	71	97
6§	5	7	5	7	6	7	5	6	5	5	4
13.6	36.8	29.8	49.3	26.9	24.0	22.1	24.5	25.6	12.0	32.3	44.8
8	6	8	2	3	7	3	7	1	1	5	7

Resources

The Climate Alliance
Umwelt Forum
Rathaus
Frankfurt
Germany

Ecological Design Association
20 High Street
Stroud
Gloucestershire GL5 1AS
England
(0453) 752985

EcoNet
3228 Sacramento Street
San Francisco
CA 94115, USA
(415) 923 0900

The Farallones Institute
55C Gate Five Road
Sausalito
CA 94965, USA
(415) 332 3267

Friends of the Earth
26-8 Underwood House
London N1 7J2
England
(071) 490 1555

GreenNet
23 Bevenden Street
London N1 6BH
England

ICLEI Liaison Office
Fehrenbachallee 12
D 7800 Freiburg
Germany

International Council for Local
Environmental Initiatives
City Hall
East Tower, 8th floor
Toronto, Ontario M5H 2N2
Canada

Mega-Cities Project
4 Washington Square North
New York University
New York, NY 10003, USA

Urban Ecology
PO Box 10144
Berkeley, California
CA 94709, USA
(415) 549 1724

WHO Regional Office for Europe
8 Scherfigsvej
DK 2100 Copenhagen
Denmark

Bibliography

Banham, R, *Los Angeles: The Architecture of Four Ecologies,* Allen Lane The Penguin Press, 1971

Benevolo, L, *The History of the City,* Scolar Press, London, 1980

Blowers, A, Hamnett, C, Sarre, P, *The Future of Cities,* Hutchinson Educational, 1974

Bookchin, M, *Towards an Ecological Society,* Black Rose Books, Montreal, 1980

Boyden, S, Millar, S, Newcombe, K, O'Neill, B, *The Ecology of a City and its People,* Australian National University Press, Canberra, 1981

Boyle, S & Ardill, J, *The Greenhouse Effect,* 1989

Briggs, A, *Victorian Cities,* Penguin Books, London, 1963

Brown, L, *State of the World 1992: A Worldwatch Institute Report on Progress Toward a Sustainable Society,* Earthscan, London, 1992

Brown, L, Flavin, C, Postel, S, *Saving the Planet: How to Shape an Environmentally Sustainable Global Economy,* W. W. Norton and Company, New York & London, 1991

Brunn, S D & Williams, J F, *Cities of the World,* Harper and Row, New York, 1983

Burger, J, *The Gaia Atlas of First Peoples,* Robertson McCarta, London, and Doubleday, New York, 1990

Cadman, D & Payne, G (eds), *The Living City,* Routledge, London, 1990

Campbell, B, *Human Ecology: The Story of Our Place in Nature from Prehistory to the Present,* Heinemann Educational Books, London, 1983

Canfield, C (ed), *Ecocity Conference 1990,* Berkeley, 1990

Carter, H, *An Introduction to Urban Historical Geography,* Arnold, London, 1983

Chesney, K, *The Victorian Underworld,* Temple Smith, London, 1970

Chisholm, M, *Rural Settlement and Land Use,* Hutchinson University Library, London, 1962

Coleman, A, *Utopia on Trial,* Hilary Shipman, 1990

Corfield, P J, *The Impact of English Towns,* Opus, London, 1982

Davidson, J, *How Green is Your City? Pioneering Approaches to Environmental Action,* Bedford Square Press, London, 1988

Davis, M, *City of Quartz,* Verso, London & New York, 1990

DeMarco, G, *A Short History of Los Angeles,* Lexicos, San Francisco, 1988

Drakakis-Smith, D, *The Third World City,* Routledge, London & New York, 1990

Ekins, P, Hillman, M & Hutchison, R, *Wealth Beyond Measure: An Atlas of New Economics,* Gaia Books, London, & Doubleday, New York, 1992

Evenson, N, *The Indian Metropolis,* Yale University Press, 1989

Fraser, D, *Village Planning in the Primitive World,* Studio Vista, London

Fuchs, R J, Jones, G W & Pernla, E M, *Urbanisation and Urban Politics in Pacific Asia,* Westview Press, 1987

Girardet, H (ed), *Land for the People,* Crescent Books, London, 1976

Girardet, H, *Earthrise,* Paladin Books, London, 1992

Gordon, D, *Green Cities: Ecologically Sound Approaches to Urban Space,* Black Rose Books, 1990

Gribbin, J, *Hothouse Earth,* Bantam Books, London, 1990

Gugler, J (ed), *The Urbanization of the Third Word,* Oxford University Press, 1988

Hall, P, *Cities of Tomorrow: An Intellectual History of Urban Planning and Design in the Twentieth Century,* Basil Blackwell, 1988

Hardoy, J, *Urban Planning in Pre-Columbian America,* Studio Vista, London, 1967

Hardoy, J, Cairncross, S & Satterthwaite, D, *The Poor Die Young,* Earthscan Publications, London, 1990

Hardoy, J E & Satterthwaite, D, *Squatter Citizen: Life in the Urban Third World,* Earthscan, London, 1989

Harvey, D, *Consciousness and the Urban Experience,* Blackwell, Oxford, 1985

Hinkle, L E & Loring, W C, *The Effect of the Man-Made Environment on Health & Behaviour,* Castle House Publications, 1979

Hough, M, *City Form and Natural Process,* Routledge, London and New York, 1984

Jack Todd, N & Todd, J, *Bioshelters, Ocean Arks, City Farming: Ecology as the Basis of Design,* Sierra Club Books, San Francisco, 1984

Jones, E, *Metropolis: The World's Great Cities,* Oxford University Press, 1990

King, A D, *Global Cities,* Routledge, London, 1990

Kohr, L, *Tract: The City as Convivial Centre,* The Gryphon Press, Cardiganshire, 1974

Lampl, P, *Cities and Planning in the Ancient Near East,* Studio Vista, London

Little, J, Peake, L, Richardson, P (eds), *Women in Cities: Gender and the Urban Environment,* Macmillan Education, London, 1988

Mayhew, H, (ed Quennell), *Mayhew's London,* Hamlyn, London, 1969

McLaughlin, C & Davidson G, *Builders of the Dawn: Changing Lifestyles in a Changing World,* Stillpoint Publishing, New Hampshire, 1985

Milne, A, *Our Drowning World,* Prism Press, 1989

Mumford, L, *The Story of Utopias: Ideal Commonwealths and Social Myths,* George Harrap, London, 1923

Mumford, L, *The City in History: Its Origins, its Transformations and its Prospects,* Penguin Books, London 1961

Murray, J (ed), *Cultural Atlas of Africa,* Phaidon, London, 1981

Myers, N, *The Gaia Atlas of Future Worlds,* Robertson McCarta, London, & Doubleday, New York, 1990

Myers, N (gen ed), *The Gaia Atlas of Planet Management,* Pan Books, London, & Doubleday, New York, 1985

Nicholson-Lord, D, *The Greening of Cities,* Routledge & Kegan Paul, London, 1987

Payne, G, *Informal Housing and Land Subdivisions in Third World Cities: A Review of the Literature,* Centre for Development and Environmental Planning, Oxford, 1989

Rapoport, A, *House Form and Culture,* Prentice-Hall, New York, 1969

Raven, S, *Rome in Africa,* Longman, London & New York, 1969

Register, R, *Ecocity Berkeley: Building Cities for a Healthy Future.* North Atlantic Press, Berkeley, California. 1987

Reisner, M, *Cadillac Desert,* Penguin, New York, 1986

Rudofsky, B, *Architecture without Architects,* Academy Editions, London, 1964

Sale, K, *Dwellers in the Land: The Bioregional Vision,* New Society Publishers, 1991

Schaffer, P, *The New Town Story,* Paladin, London, 1972

Seager, J, *The State of the Earth: An Atlas of Environmental Concern,* Unwin Hyman, 1990

Sennett, R, *The Uses of Disorder,* Penguin, London, 1970

Seymour, J & Girardet, H, *Blueprint for a Green Planet,* Dorling Kindersley, London, 1989

Seymour, J & Girardet, H, *Far From Paradise,* Green Books, London, 1989

Sharpe, W & Wallock, L, *Visions of the Modern City,* John Hopkins University Press, 1987

Sherlock, H, *Cities are Good for Us:* Transport 2000, London, 1990

Short, J R, *The Humane City,* Basil Blackwell, Oxford, 1989

Smith, P F, *Architecture and the Human Dimension,* Eastview Editions, Inc., New Jersey, 1979

Tanghe, J et al, *Living Cities,* Pergamon Press, London, 1984

Thompson, E P, *The Making of the English Working Class,* Penguin, London, 1982

Toynbee, A, *Cities of Destiny,* Thames & Hudson, London, 1968

Turner, B (ed), *Building Community,* HABITAT, 1988

Ward, C, *The Child in the City,* Bedford Sqare Press, London, 1978

Ward, C, *Welcome Thinner City,* Bedford Square Press, London, 1989

Van der Ryn, S & Calthorpe, P, *Sustainable Communities: A New Design Synthesis for Cities, Suburbs and Towns,* Sierra Club Books, San Francisco, 1968

Vance, J E, *Urban Morphology in Western Civilization,* John Hopkins University Press, Baltimore & London, 1990

Walmsley, J E, *Urban Living,* Longman, London, 1988

Weightman, G & Humphries, S, *The Making of Modern London,* Sidgwick & Jackson, London, 1983

White, P, *The West European City,* Longman, London, 1984

Wrigley, E A, *People, Cities and Wealth,* Blackwell, Oxford, 1987

Whyte, W H, *City: Rediscovering the Centre,* Doubleday, New York, 1988

A Green City Program For San Francisco Bay Area Cities and Towns, Planet Drum Books, San Francisco, 1989

Global Report on Human Settlements 1986, United Nations Centre for Human Settlements (HABITAT)

"Cities: Life in the World's 100 Largest Metropolitan Areas", Population Crisis Committee, Washington DC, 1990

Index

A

Abercrombie, Patrick 58
Acid rain 110
Agglomerations 71
Air circulation, and urban temperature 28
Alberti, Leone Battista 46
Allotments 136, 138
Aluminium production 98
~ and recycling 153
Amsterdam, and car-free plan 150
Ancient cities 40, 42-3
Athens, and air pollution 28

B

Babylon, and environmental decline 22
Balbina dam, Brazil 91
Baltic Sea, and pollution of 100
Bangkok, and child-selling, prostitution 78
Bauhaus 65
Berlin, and city layout 52, 121
~ and recycling 154
~ see also Kreuzberg
Bhopal disaster 96
Bicycles 146, 147
Biocidic cities 22, 166
Biogenic cities 22
Bioregionalism 160
Black Country, England 50-1
Bombay, and shanties 75
~ and Child-to-Child scheme 135
Bomb damage, and building 60
Brasilia, and Le Corbusier 56
~ and cars 104
British Empire 48-9
Broadacre City 62-3
Brunelleschi 47

C

Calcutta, and colonial origins 48
~ "Concern for Calcutta" campaign 158
Carbon dioxide (CO_2) emissions 24, 28, 29, 36, 37, 102, 142, 145, 166, 167
Carbon monoxide (CO) emissions 102
Carnivals 118, 126-7
Cars 24, 102-5, 132
~ and influence on planning 62, 146
~ and low-density city layouts 104, 106
Cathal Huyuk 38
Ceaucescu 60
Chandigarh, and Le Corbusier 56
Children, and poverty 78
Chinese cities
~ and air pollution 108
~ and ecological viability 23

~ and history of 38
~ and sewage recycling 162
Christiania, Copenhagen 124-5
Circular metabolism 23, 24-5, 156, 166, 169
City centre 118, 120
City layout 24
Clean Air Act 1955, 108
Climate Alliance 167
Climate protection 166
Coal production and industrialization 50
Co-disposal, of waste 98, 152
Co-housing 173
Colonialism 47, 48-9, 50
Combined Heat and Power 142-3
ComLink 36
Community, sense of 118, 122-3, 138
~ see also Christiania
~ and Medieval cities
~ and self-help housing
Compact cities 170, 172
Composting, human waste 52
Constantinople, and origins 46
Crack, and inner cities 84
Crime, and poverty 78, 82
"Crystal" cities 62-3
Curitiba, and surface metro 150

D

Dams, and water supply to cities 90-1
Davis, California, and sustainability 170-1
Deforestation 38, 42, 71, 88-9
Density, urban population 22, 73, 146
Depression, The 62
De-zoning 146
Dinkelsbühl, and layout 44-5
Diseases
~ and antibiotics in food production 92
~ and car exhaust fumes 108
~ and industrial threat 96
~ and leacheate 100
~ and poverty, overcrowding, and squalor 50
~ and stagnant water 90, 91
~ and stress 82, 84
Dresden, and bombing 60

E

Eco-cities 156-7
EcoNet 36
Egyptians, Ancient 39
"Electronic homes" 172, 174
Emissions, from cars 102
Energy
~ and consumption by cities 28, 36, 142
~ household 144-5
~ responsible systems 23-4

~ and supply to cities 24, 38
~ sustainability 132
~ and taxation 168
~ and wastage 106
Environmental
~ damage by cities 22, 34
~ decline 42
~ instability of cities 42
European Climate Alliance 166
European Commission's Task Force on the Environment 104

F

Farms, urban 136, 140
Favelas 74
Feedback systems 157
Fertility and human waste 162
Financial power, of cities 34
Firewood supply, to cities 22
Florence, and Renaissance 46-7, 118
Food supply, to cities 22, 32, 38, 48, 92-3
~ city self-sufficiency 162, 168
~ and pesticides 92
~ and waste 98
Forest
~ and air pollution damage 108-11
~ and cities' responsibility 24
~ and cover 88
~ and depletion 38
~ and protection 166
Fossil fuel use, and cities 23, 86, 106, 142, 166, 170
Free cities, medieval 40, 44
French Revolution 52
Fuel efficiency 146
Fuel supply, to cities 48
Fuelwood crisis, India 89

G

Gaia 20
Gangs 70, 84-5
Garden Cities 54-5, 56, 58, 136, 170
GlasNet 36
Glass recycling 154
Global village 20, 37
Global warming 24, 112, 167, 170
Globalopolis 20, 37
Greater London Plan 58
Green belt 54, 58
Greenhouse gases 28, 29, 156, 166
Greening, of cities 132, 136, 138, 173
GreenNet 36
Green spaces 30, 132, 138, 174
Gridlock, traffic 132, 148
Gropius, Walter 56
Guilds, medieval 44

Author's acknowledgements

The creation of this book was a complicated process. Much of it was written in the hills of South Wales: London was at the end of a telephone line. But, one day, my editors caught me by the scruff of the neck and tied me to a chair in their London office, where they kept me until the book was done. Bird song was replaced by the sounds of drills, sirens, dot matrix printers. We all survived and a book was born.

The Gaia Atlas of Cities emerged out of the collaboration of a wonderful team of people. In some ways it was like making a documentary film; trying to achieve a union of images and text. I, for one, feel, that it might be timelessly relevant for some years to come.

I am indebted to Joss Pearson, a uniquely creative publisher, for asking me to write a book which had been stewing in my mind for some years. I am also thankful to David Pearson and John F.C. Turner, both of whom read the manuscript and suggested ways of refining the text argument, based on their rich experience and pioneering contribution as community planners and architects.

I am deeply indebted to Joanna Godfrey Wood, the editor of this book, who stayed patient with me as its shape slowly evolved, and coped with my frequent mind changes with good humour. Fiona Trent and Suzy Boston both contributed their own good sense and intellectual commitment as the text took its final shape over several slow months.

I am grateful to Patrick Nugent for brilliantly conceiving the initial designs that evolved into the illustrations. Simon Adamczewski took up the baton, developed the ideas and commissioned the artwork with great skill and flair. Thank you very much. I also wish to thank the illustrators, Darrel Rees, Richard Jenkins, Matthew Cooper, Paul Davis, and Robert Omodiagbe for their imaginative artwork. Special thanks to Mark Edwards for taking photos for the book and my thanks to Susan Mennell for scouring the world's photo libraries for further suitable photos. Thanks also to Sara Mathews who worked on the design in the early stages. I want to thank everybody at Gaia Books who came and fed me chocolate, bread and water as I sat tied to my office chair.

There are many people on whose work I have drawn and who are only credited in the bibliography and the resources section. I particularly wish to thank David Satterthwaite, Janice Perlman, David Hall, Peter de la Cour, and Colin Ward, who helped me with source material. I want to thank Chris Wilbert for researching and collating material from many different sources.

My wife Barbara and my sons Alexis and Stefan put up with my unsteady moods and my mental and physical absences during the writing of this book. Thank you for your great patience, your good advice and your love!

Publisher's acknowledgements

Gaia Books would like to thank the following for their help in the production of this book: John F.C. Turner, David Pearson, Philip Parker, Eva Webster, and Janine Christley for editorial advice, research, and development; Mark Edwards for special photography in Mexico City; Lesley Gilbert for copy preparation; Phil Gamble for design development; Susan Walby for production; Chris Wilbert for research; Joe Wood for statistics; and thanks to Gill Smith, Samantha Nunn, Imogen Bright, and Libby Hoseason.

Printed by Craft Print Pte, Singapore
Reproduction by Well-Tech, Colour
Separation Limited, Hong Kong
Typeset by Tradespools Ltd, Frome, UK

Illustration credits

Darrel Rees: cover, 18/19, 21, 38/39, 66/67, 68/69, 90/91, 116/117, 132/133
Matthew Cooper: 22/23, 24/25, 49, 83, 118/119, 122/123, 128/129, 152/153, 163
Paul Davis: 28/29, 60/61, 101, 112/113, 156/157

Richard Jenkins: 32/33, 34/35, 42/43, 64/65, 76/77, 92/93, 99, 102/103, 114/115, 142/143, 164/165, 168/169
Robert Omodiagbe: 72/73, 86/87, 94/95, 136/137, 147

Diagram pp. 160-1 source: Chisholm, M, *Rural Resettlement and Land Use*, Hutchinson University Library, London, 1962

Diagram pp. 164-5 source: Dr William Sopper, "Forests as Living Filters for Urban Sewage", Gordon, D (ed), *Green Cities: Ecologically Sound Approaches to Urban Spaces,* Black Rose Books, 1990

Photographic credits

Key: b = bottom, t = top, l = left, r = right, m = main picture, i = inset picture

Arcaid p. 65 (Richard Bryant)
Bruce Coleman pp. 12 b (Henneghien), 126-7 (Luiz Claudio Marigo), 150-1 (John Waters)
Commission for New Towns pp. 58-9
Explorer p. 53
First Garden City Heritage Museum, Letchworth Garden City p. 55 tl
© 1958 Flwright Fdn p. 63 b
Herbert Girardet pp. 145, 170-1
Jimmy Holmes pp. 63 t, 155
Magnum Photos p. 81 (Peter Marlow), 176-7 (Raymond Depardon)
Dieter Magnus pp. 140-1
Mansell Collection p. 51 t
Network Photographers pp. 8-9 (Barry Lewis), 85 (Drexel/Bilderberg), 114-15 (Barry Lewis), 125 t (Chris Davis), 175 (Didier Ruef), 178-9 (Barry Lewis)
Popperfoto pp. 56-7 i
Reflections Photo Library pp. 31-2 (Martin Dohrn)
Retna Pictures pp. 180-1 (Steve Rapport)
Science Photo Library pp. 106-7 (Roger Ressmeyer/Starlight), 110-11 i (CNRI)
Mark Edwards/Still Pictures pp. 10, 56-7 m (Jorgen Schytte), 74-5, 76-7, 78-9, 97, 98-9, 109, 125 b, 130-1, 138-9, 161
Verkehrsamt der Stadt Dinkelsbuhl pp. 44-5
Welwyn Garden City Central Library pp. 55 tr and b
Zefa Picture Library pp. 12 t, 14-15, 17, 20-1, 46-7, 104-5, 110-11 m

ALSO PUBLISHED BY GAIA

For a complete list of titles published by Gaia Books, write to or telephone Gaia Books, 20 High Street, Stroud, Gloucestershire, GL5 1AS Tel 01453 752985 Fax 01453 752987

Gaia: The practical science of planetary medicine

James Lovelock

ISBN 1 85675 040 X   £16.99

Lovelock has changed our view of the world. This book addresses planetary health, diagnosis of its sickness, prognosis for recovery and presciptions for treatment.

"Lovelock is a brilliant writer" *New Scientist*

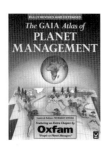

The Gaia Atlas of Planet Management

Fully revised and extended with a new illustrated chapter by OXFAM

General Editor Norman Myers

ISBN 1 85675 061 2   £16.99

Planet Management involves taking an informed, global look at the activities that affect people and the planet, and planning for the future. This book sets the agenda for the ecology movement.

Wealth Beyond Measure

An atlas of new economics

Paul Ekins

ISBN 1 85675 050 7   £9.99

Create a healthy, sustainable and humane society where money and economic growth are not the main aim. The book illustrates how co-operation at a local level can really help create equality of wealth and health.

The Natural Garden Book

Peter Harper, Jeremy Light and Chris Madsen

ISBN 1 85675 056 6   £14.99 PAPERBACK

This is no ordinary gardening book. It is a fresh, practical and inspiring guide to creating a productive, healthy, garden. With detailed drawings, checklists and instructions, for planning and daily practice. Learn to use toxin-free techniques and encourage wildlife into your garden.

The Natural Hedgehog

Lenni Sykes with Jane Durrant

ISBN 1 85675 042 6   £8.99 HARDBACK

A highly illustrated guide to making your garden hedgehog friendly, and looking after sick or injured hedgehogs. The Natural Hedgehog aims to balance the threat to hedgehogs from transport and pesticides with homeopathic healing and other holistic treatments for the casualties.